9-3-80

A
SECOND DAY

Books by Robert Farrar Capon

A
SECOND DAY

REFLECTIONS
ON REMARRIAGE

BY ROBERT FARRAR CAPON

WILLIAM MORROW AND COMPANY, INC.
New York   1980

Library of Congress Cataloging in Publication Data

Capon, Robert Farrar.
    A second day.

    Includes index.
    1. Remarriage—United States.   I. Title.
HQ1018.S4C33   306.8'7   80-15750
ISBN 0-688-03680-X

Printed in the United States of America

First Edition

1 2 3 4 5 6 7 8 9 10

BOOK DESIGN BY MICHAEL MAUCERI

CONTENTS

PREFACE

On the one hand,

We marry for the wrong reasons and get divorced for the right ones (Alan Jay Lerner, to a daughter seeking marital advice);

on the other hand,

Whosoever putteth away his wife and marrieth another committeth adultery (Jesus, to some Pharisees who thought he was a liberal);

and, to make matters even worse,

Divorce is not a wrong, it is a metaphysical impossibility (myself, fifteen years ago);

however,

It is also theoretically impossible, in a three-dimensional system, to turn your socks inside out (a science teacher, thirty-five years ago).

In view of which,

Impossibility is hardly the last word on anything; death is (myself, three years ago).

Now then, since

Death is a lot simpler than arguing about who's to blame for it (overheard outside Suffolk County Supreme Court, Special Term, Part V),

9

and because

There must be love in a novel (Anthony Trollope),

but above all because

There is therefore now no condemnation (St. Paul to the Romans),

the one thing that seems clear is that

"All of the above" is the only answer that just might not be completely wrong (Mrs. Murphy).

So much for the fruits of thirty-five years of research for this book. After all this time, I find myself more concerned with the human beings committed to marriage, divorce and remarriage than I am with those grand predicaments themselves. Not that there aren't many things, pro and con, that I still have to say about the subjects; it's just that now, having myself been chin-deep in all three, I am less enchanted than I used to be with good advice. We do not need so much to be told what's best to do, as to be assured that, right or wrong, we stand on something more solid than the quicksand of our own intentions. Bits of advice do indeed appear in this book, but only, as it were, in the accompaniment; the melody is a hymn to forgiveness and resurrection—to the grace that builds whether we do or not.

One disclaimer, and we're on our way. There are no references to persons here—myself included—which are not to some degree fictionalized. It has not been my intention to produce a resemblance of anybody, living or dead—only to write a love letter to everyone I ever knew. Besides, in the resurrection, we shall all have new faces; our true pictures are there, not here. Relax, therefore; our good looks are in the best possible hands.

ROBERT FARRAR CAPON

Shelter Island, New York 1980

A
SECOND DAY

I

A SECOND DAY

Join me, if you will. It is a perfectly still, late Indian summer morning and I am flat on my back contemplating the mystery of marriage. Well, not quite flat. Tilted, head downward, is more like it: I am in what medical institutions call the Trendelenburg position—on a knoll behind the fourteenth green of a golf course. And it's not exactly marriage I'm out here to think about: I have spent thirty years at it, all told, but the precise position I'm in now as far as that institution is concerned is remarriage. All of which leaves me, I suppose, not at right angles to anything. But not to worry. Find yourself a patch of grass and stretch out.

Why do I pick this place? Because I stop here every morning whether I have large subjects to think about or not. Halfway through my five-mile run, I take a siesta. The shirtier members of the jogging fraternity, with their religion of fancy shoes and stopwatches, take a dim view of my lollygagging, but I have better things to do than compete in their league. I wear old sneakers and refuse to clock myself. The way I see it, we'll all be clothed with the earth longer than with anything else, so if I take time out once a day to check the fit, it's twenty minutes well spent.

Besides, the runner's mind empties itself when it rests. Or, better said, it stops trying to jam ideas into line and lets them drift through as they like. That's why I haven't gotten around to the mystery just yet. Something more noticeable has drifted in ahead of it: the utter quietness here.

We are on an island between the two forks of eastern Long Island. Seen from the air, it is only a hundred miles from New York City; but as the ear perceives it today, it's hardly in the same world. The silence here is something the urban mind never even imagines. It is not negative, not a mere absence of surface sounds: the odd chirp, bark, rustle or rifle crack does indeed erupt, but without disturbing the quiet at all. Rather it is positive: the presence, behind all those sounds, of no subsurface noise at all—of a baffle so infinite and so perfect that it becomes the first thing the ear notices. And if it is unheard of in the city, it is still not all that common here. On most days, if I listen closely, what I hear in the background is simply other sound: a truck changing gears on the North Fork, an oyster dragger laboring up the channel, the interminable snarl of light aircraft, the distant rumble of jets.

But today, for a few minutes at least, there is none of that. And while it lasts, I play a game of daring the silence to disclose itself—of invoking the deep stillness that even nature only occasionally allows and which the internal combustion engine has almost abolished for good. I peel back the successive silences like the layers of an onion, always challenging the next one to be more perfect than the last. If the bay is quiet, I defy the wind to speak. If the wind stays still, I command the cars to be silent. If they obey me, I forbid planes. And when, pushing my luck but scarcely believing in it, I dare the jets and they too decline, I put a commemorative notch in my mind: I have heard the nothing out of which God made the world; on a day like this, even I might come up with something.

At first, though, it isn't much. The next impression that wanders in is of gulls defacing the silence with audible graffiti. They fill the air with complaints, not because they're justified but because they're habitual complainers. They certainly eat well enough. Scalloping is the main winter industry here and the town dump for the shucked remains is half a mile up the road. It's no place for human beings to be downwind of on a hot day, but the gulls don't mind it. Through all the months with r's they stuff themselves with the nine-tenths of the mollusk that man in his fastidiousness throws away. Morning after morning they wheel and screech straight over my head, working off the first of what must be thirty meals a day. Maybe they're not complaining. Maybe they're laughing at me for paying nine dollars a quart to provide them with free breakfasts. Who knows? I let it pass and listen again.

The silence is still there, but other voices rasp against its surface: crows out of the woods. They act as if they own this place. They rent it out in the summer to red-winged blackbirds; but in the fall they reclaim their territory like loudmouthed landlords comparing notes on the depredations of their tenants. With songbirds, man can manage the conceit that he is somehow included in their conversation. But not with crows. Their talk is strictly to each other. They take over the countryside the way real estate operators take over a restaurant at lunchtime: they flap through, talking easements over their shoulders, and no one else can hear himself think. I decide to wait till they're gone before I even try.

Something catches my eye, though. I have my glasses off to keep them from steaming up, so sounds have gotten all my attention so far. But even in soft focus, the lone bird with the wide wings registers well enough. As big as a herring gull, but higher in the sky, he has a banking, squared-off glide pattern that gives him away. I'm almost positive, but I put on the glasses to make sure. And it is. An osprey.

What's he doing here, though? I'd have thought they'd all be gone by now. But then, who am I to say? I'm not supposed to be here either. Not being a member of this club, I am persona non grata to the head groundsman who chases me off unless I outwit him. Hence my position (down, out of sight) and my attention to sounds (he patrols his domain on a power mower). The osprey's justification for being here is the same as mine. Neither of us has consulted the authorities about our plans for the season. We have no permission slips; only reasons of our own.

The mind clicks. Does anyone really have more than that? We act, of course, as if we should. We worry endlessly about whether we're legitimate in other people's eyes, but all that does is scare us out of being the protagonists of our own lives. The osprey is lucky. He can't hear the chorus of experts telling him where to head in, so he's not tempted to let them decide for him. But we hear them. And we're more than tempted: we let their pronouncements intimidate us to the point of paralysis. We stop ourselves in mid-flight and then wonder why we fell out of the sky.

Legitimacy is no substitute for having the wind in your wings. Our respective choruses, whether they approve of us or not, will not and cannot act for us. But it's easy to forget that, especially when they approve. If I'm told my marriage is somehow all right, what does that do but trick me into thinking I've got more help with it than I really do—into imagining that life, or fate, or God is going to take over for me? But nothing can, really. God sends his rain on the just and the unjust alike. Brownie points have a cash value of zero.

It's illegitimacy, therefore, that turns out to be the supportive proposition. It's when I'm told that my marriage is all wrong that I am most clearly reminded I'm the only one who can make it work. And not only is this realistic, it's also attractive. I've lived on this island for three years now—almost as long as I've been remarried—and I find myself running a kind of safe house for illegitimate types. What attracts them in particular, I think, is not just the prospect of company in misery; much more, it's the spectacle of two purported outcasts in no rush to get back to respectability.

Admittedly, it's a modest spectacle. Madeleine and I are lawfully married—for whatever that's worth when her push comes to my shove—and we have rugs on the floor. The criminality of our alliance has been, by any objective standard, exaggerated. But since we have neither overrated the legality nor denied the crime, there remains a patina of illegitimacy on us. People blinded by the high polish of righteousness apparently find us easy on the eyes.

But you and I have plenty of time, so the details of all that—gorgeous, prurient or drab—can wait a bit. I see you as a visitor to my safe house: the old-fashioned kind who brackets a whole day with two nights spent under his host's roof. This is your second day—let's make it a Saturday, if we may—and it's ours to spend as we like: on the mystery, to be sure; but on whatever else comes to hand as well. We shall talk and cook and eat and drink our way through a day off in the country. The only thing we shall not do is hurry back to legitimacy.

Still, though, let's finish this opening exercise and head for home before the groundsman and his exhaust-belcher defile the silence—and, God forbid, before he gets a chance to deliver one of his lectures on illegality. We don't need him spreading gloom all over what may be our salvation.

Anyway, illegitimacy is *my* subject.

II

DIS-QUALIFICATIONS

We're back. Help yourself to a cup of coffee while I make some toast. Madeleine may not be visible yet, but she's produced her usual brew from fresh-ground beans so we may as well enjoy it. Smells like Haitian, but I wouldn't want to swear to it. When it comes to her morning cup, Madeleine is practically the first of the big spenders: we have about nine varieties, and she's not above doing on-the-spot blending of her own. It's always good though. I'm spoiled. I haven't had to drink instant powdered floor varnish for years.

Where precisely is Madeleine at the moment? Once again, her ways defy unqualified prediction, but if I had to guess, I would say she's probably running in place in the bedroom. She tried running outdoors with me once for about a week, but gave it up. We seize the front end of the day better if we do it separately. Some differences are best left unreconciled. God may have promised that the lion and the lamb would lie down together in the peaceable kingdom, but he was wise enough to leave it at that: Scripture is silent about the lark and the owl getting up together. Energy and high spirits at six in the morning are her idea of hell. And when you add in the fact that she's terrified of loose dogs, you will see why joint jogging never got off the grounds we live on. It wasn't a total loss, though. At least this way, the coffee's always ready when I get back.

But you have other questions, I'm sure. Even though I've just gotten through praising the quietness, you're tempted to ask: isn't it awfully quiet here? Doesn't living on an island accessible only by ferry get . . . well, insular? How do we put groceries on the table out here in the drink? What's it like in the winter? Don't people become desperate to get off? What on earth do they do for entertainment?

Let me answer you in no particular order. Insularity? Oh, my, yes. If you take a small town and surround it with water you get more than insularity; you get the pure essence of parochialism. And if you cover it with snow, you get almost nothing else. Actually, it's not scalloping that's the principal winter industry here; if you know which nineteen-hundred out of the two thousand year-round residents to sidle up to, it turns out to be gossip and character assassination. The low hum of that goes on no matter how quiet things get.

Desperation to get off? Again, yes. The local name for it is Rock Fever. Even the character assassins have an occasional case of it when they tire of their entertainments, but their victims have it worse. Oddly enough, though, the preferred treatment is not leaving the island; it's being patient enough till springtime comes and everybody turns rumps together, horns out against the summer people. Nothing like an invasion to make your homeland precious.

But how do we manage to put groceries on the table?

Ah, that one takes a little more answering. In the loose, large sense, Madeleine and I survive because people give us money for what they are kind enough to consider services. But if you want a finer point on it, you will have to put up with some details. Over the past months, for example, we have catered a few weddings and luncheons. The precise financial exercise involved in that is keeping expenses below one-third of the price we quote. We have succeeded, I think, just once. Next time we'll quote higher.

That, thank God and Madeleine, is not our whole living. She is currently supporting her coffee habit by renting my typewriter, her services and her son's bedroom to a nonprofit group dedicated to saving wetlands. (I, in grateful return, do all the household cooking, thus providing her with what every working woman needs most: a wife. We congratulate ourselves on having achieved the ultimate improvement in matrimonial relations: the husbandless marriage.)

Nonprofit, however, is just about what we make from all that, so further exertions are necessary on my part: for the rest, I am a writer. What that means in practice is that I work odd hours and survive (so far) by means of a symbiotic relationship with an agent. I send him quantities of double-spaced typing and he in turn sends me nine-tenths of what, if anything, other people pay him for it. This arrangement (known either as free-lancing, or taking out a license to starve) has in the past few years produced two cookbooks of my own, two rewrites for other authors, a monthly newspaper column of advice to the foodlorn, a chronically declining bank balance and a good many wee hours spent wondering how low on the hog you can eat without falling off.

If those employments strike you as somewhat less than honest labor, they sometimes do me too. It is in the gainless spaces between them that I do what I consider real work. Every author without a signed contract in his desk works on a novel. I differ from the rest only in that I am, and have been for years, working on three novels, none of which has shown the least interest in passing GO. Still, for sheer dog-work, there is nothing like hurling creative fiats at the rich chaos of your own experience and coming up, invariably, with zilch. If I were a cynic, I would be bitter about the discrepancy between effort and reward. But since I never believed in a correspondence between the two anyway—and since the system, if there is one, seems determined to pay me only for having fun—who am I to complain?

There are only three other services for which the whimsical powers that be have seen fit to remunerate me. As to the first: certain publishers from time to time send me mysterious checks in amounts like $21.43, $37.58 and $61.01. These, they claim, are the current fruits of books I wrote in a previous existence. (They also, and more often, send me equally puzzling statements to the effect that they have not sold enough other books of mine to warrant any payments over the original advance.)

As to the second: there is a small consortium of American businesses (Ma Bell, Westinghouse, PSE&G of I forget where, and others too marginal to mention) who, in return for the use of some family capital badly damaged by four trips through probate and one through the divorce court, regularly mail me tokens of appreciation. These amount, in the aggregate, to just under four months' rent money. If the sum is not princely, it at least makes it possible to work the occasional can of smoked oysters into the food budget.

The third service? Ah, yes. At one time—for the better part of three decades, in fact—the Church paid me for teaching and preaching the Gospel. This pleasant, if medieval arrangement, however, came to an abrupt end three years ago when, on the occasion of my divorce and remarriage, I made the mistake of placing for myself an order of what they had been asking me to sell.

The firm did indeed deal in forgiveness, they assured me, but my order was for a size they unfortunately did not have in stock. I tried to find out why. Had the old, one-size-fits-all number been discontinued? Were the new, proportioned models delayed in shipment? Could I call on Thursday? They said no, but that if they ever located any, they would phone me the minute it got in. In the meantime, they suggested, perhaps I would like six months' severance pay and some therapy instead.

The combination struck me as odd. The offer of therapy seemed to imply an interest in my future, but the demand for a resignation indicated an unfortunate preoccupation with my past. Since I myself had not exactly dealt triumphantly with either of those times, I decided not to leave them—or my present, either—in more confused hands than my own. I wrote the letter, took the money, declined the treatment and walked out the window.

The drop, as you can see, was not fatal, though it did seem like a long while before I came to rest. When I finally did, I was on this island. And, since time seemed to be the one thing we had plenty of, I found myself paying not only more, but different attention to it. For one thing, clock time is almost an irrelevancy here. There's no point, for example, in trying to go running at 5:30 A.M. in January. There are no street lights: it's so dark you could—and I almost did—break an ankle. Once I realized that, I gave up setting alarms and got up with the light instead.

I shifted, in other words, from the habit of asking what time it was to the saner procedure of asking what it was time for. When that sank in as far as running was concerned, I decided to apply it to the rest of what goes on here as well. The way we arrange a day is to determine what jobs need doing and set an order for doing them. Then we follow the order till they're finished and go to bed. I recommend the arrangement. It's not only productive; the best thing about it is that it gets things done without letting them ride roughshod over the human beings involved.

For instance, take yesterday. What I had to do was: run, have a kaffeeklatsch with Madeleine, shower, write, have a teaklatsch with Madeleine, write, shop, cook supper, eat it and talk to you. In my old life, I would have set times for each of these activities and fidgeted my way through most of them because the clock kept threatening me with the next one. Here, however, I just pay attention to what's at hand.

It makes, not only for better work, but for variety as well. Morning coffee time is free to be a one-cup business meeting or a two-pot soul baring; the writing goes on, not for a certain number of hours, but till I have finished—or decisively despaired of—what I started out to do. Practically the only thing I use the clock for is figuring out when to begin making bread. Only a single calculation is involved: it must be started six hours ahead of serving. But even there, I can take my pick: make the bread for dinner at six; or eat at eight because I didn't start till two.

You object, no doubt, that only writers and other layabouts can sit loose to the clock like that, but I refuse to agree with you. True enough, if you work nine to five for somebody else, you're stuck—but only for those hours. The sad thing about most people is that they go right on clockwatching even on their own time. At the very least, they should take a vow not to know what time it is on Saturdays or Sundays. If time is money, then it operates under the same rule: if you have to ask, you can't afford it. In either case, until you're able to thumb your nose at the bookkeeping department, you'll never feel like J. P. Morgan.

We are back, you see, at the saving subject of illegitimacy again—at my pet idea that it's precisely our disqualifications for conventional living that constitute our qualifications for real life. And not because the conventions haven't got a skin of reason on them. They do. Punctuality, fiscal responsibility and moral respectability are all neat ideas. Unfortunately, we're sometimes not as neat as they are— and when we're not, the habit of making them the test of our actions leaves us dead in the water. The skin of reason turns out to be a suit of armor: it's when you haven't got it on that you're most likely to make the effort to swim for your life.

But have another cup of coffee while I do something with eggs. I have a few more ideas about time, especially as it applies to divorce and remarriage, and I'd like to try them out on you. Besides having gotten myself unhooked from the clock, I think I may actually have gotten off square one on the subject of the past and future. Just to give us a little future to deal with right now, though, you name the style. What'll it be? Omelets, scrambled, boiled or over easy?

Cheese omelets, you say? Cheddar, Jarlsberg or Gruyère? Gruyère? With pepper sauce or without?

With? And how about parsley?

You think it's easy to come in here and order a future?

III

MARRIAGE, THE FUTURE & THE PAST

 As far as I've been able to figure it out—partly on my own, but also with the help of the matrimonial disaster victims who've come through here—we assign the blame for marital difficulties to the wrong part of the time spectrum. Our wretched presents are not simply the results of things that went wrong in the past; what really causes them is the loss of a proper grip on the future.

The past, after all, is simply a collection of old presents that happen not to be here any more—a mixed bag of events, more or less unreconciled, over which we no longer have even the minimal control we had while they were happening. Marriages don't thrive because they have good pasts or collapse because they have had bad ones. All marriages have both kinds, just as they have both kinds of presents as well. The ones that survive do so because they have something qualitatively different from either of those two categories. They have a future.

And not just in the sense of events whose occurrences the partners can look forward to. Viewed that way, the future is simply a today that hasn't turned up yet. Worse yet, the minute it gets here, it promptly becomes one more inaccessible yesterday. What the happily married have that's different is a future that isn't treated as just another time to come, but rather is deliberately made operative in the time that's here. They understand that the future—at least insofar as it's an engine of happiness—is a vision of a better, reconciled order. And they don't wait for its day to come: they trust it now, and they act out their trust by making its order the governing consideration in their lives now.

I first started thinking about that after we had entertained two sets of houseguests on the same weekend. The first couple were in the throes of both courtship and divorce at the same time—illegitimate types admittedly, if you go by ordinary standards, but enjoying it mightily. Their calendar future was totally unclear, but it didn't matter. They had rediscovered a believed future in their present relationship with each other and, in the light of that, had been able to see that it was just such a future they had failed to keep in their first marriages. There were howls of disapproval when they flouted the correct sequence and began living together before their divorces were final, but having caught the wind of a fresh future in their wings, they were not about to wait for anybody else's approval to fly. Right or wrong, at least they didn't make that mistake twice.

The second couple, on the other hand, were lawfully divorced and remarried. For several years, in fact. They had worked hard to achieve their legitimacy, but in spite of their success at getting the future to arrive, nothing was clearer than that the freshness of it had already slipped into the past. The only present hope they could offer the first couple was that the "inconvenience" of their illegitimacy would pass and that some day people would stop picking on them. To do her credit, the wife said she did envy them their romance, and she allowed herself a few moments of nostalgia for the days when she was in the same condition. But, she said, that always passes. Enjoy it while you can.

When they'd gone, we talked about them. What happens to people? Was it only a matter of time before couple number one came back with couple number two's speeches in their pockets? Would the same thing happen to us? And if so, why? Or was there a way to avoid it? And if so, how?

I said I thought the basic mistake was parking the future in the future instead of the present. That was what the second couple had done. At the beginning, no doubt, they got it right: their first view of their future had to have been more than just something to be waited for. And for as long as they weren't free to marry, they probably relished it, quite correctly, in each other and in the present. But when they were finally able to look forward to events to come—to a divorce date, a wedding date, a moving date— the mislocation began. The habit of waiting for the future to happen—a habit they had kicked for a while at least— came back as strong as ever.

Madeleine thought it was odd that remarried people should do that. You could understand it in first marriages, she said, especially young ones. The couples haven't lived long enough to recognize the catch in "when we're married," and "when we have a home of our own." But the remarried have seen all sorts of futures like that arrive and contribute nothing to either making or saving a life. You'd think that even if they didn't know how to celebrate the future in the present, they'd at least get a little sceptical about just waiting for it.

I proposed that even if you explained it to them, they

misunderstood. They assumed you were talking about "living in the present"—about giving up on both the past and the future and simply letting today be today. But that, as far as I was concerned, was just silly. First of all, you had very little choice about today. By and large, it would be whatever it damn well pleased. The trick was not to let it be, but to find some way of making it bearable. Besides, suggesting that people ought to live only in the present was telling them to live like animals, not human beings.

The future is a human invention. A dog or cat has a future only in the sense that if he lasts long enough, next Friday will, without having the least influence on his life in the meantime, eventually become today. Man is the only creature who thinks about the future now. So if he's to be true to his uniqueness, *now* is the place he's got to keep the future in. He's free of course, to picture it to himself in terms of *then*; but if it's to count as a reality in his life, he's got to respond to it today. If he just waits for it to arrive, he makes himself into nothing but a dog who's too smart to be happy: the future, imagined solely as an event to come, can never be more than iffy; the longer he thinks about it that way, the more likely he is to break out in cold sweats at 3 A.M.

But if he thinks of it as something whose purpose is to transform the present—to suffuse it with an effective trust in a better order—worry has a harder time getting its foot in the door. If you schedule a party for next Saturday, you don't just sit and wait for it to happen. You let it govern your attitude for all the days of preparation in between. You're never certain before the fact whether it will be a great party or not, but you allow it to give you a great time in the meanwhile. The party itself could even be canceled at the last minute—turn suddenly into no temporal future at all—and still have functioned like a true future all week.

For another thing, I said, think of Christmas. There's

no possibility of its being canceled, but something worse often happens: it comes, and it's a downer. We act surprised at that, but we shouldn't. The most dependable thing about a holiday is not the feast itself but the way it transforms the time before it. The clergy sometimes knock the secular custom of Christmasing everybody to death the minute Thanksgiving is over, but they miss the point. Advent, whether in the worldly style or the religious one, is almost the best example of the future put to its proper use. The pious, who perfume the December air with cinnamon, cardamom and clove, and the secularists who fill it with Rudolph the Red-nosed Reindeer, are both doing the same thing: suffusing the present with actions that only the believed order of the future can account for.

That's why, incidentally, Thanksgiving is seldom as big a disappointment as Christmas. Even if it's mistakenly approached as a mere time to come, the curse is taken off it by the fact that when it arrives, it comes as a day with a built-in future—namely, Christmas—already at work. December twenty-fifth, unfortunately, has no such luck: the gloom of New Year's day, the rest of winter and all of Lent are hardly prospects to transfigure any day. That's also why Thanksgiving may be an exception to the statistics that show a rise in the incidence of deaths after holidays. Misconceived futures—merely temporal ones, future futures for which we only wait—are killers: they turn out invariably to be futureless presents. Creatures who live by hope can mess with them only at their peril.

The avoidance of future futures, we decided, was the lesson to be learned from, and by, our two couples. The first part of it was negative: don't ever put off working on the future now. Its real purpose is to drive the present; postponing action on it to a time more certain almost always brings what you have in mind dangerously close to a halt. We thought of a couple who, for one reason or another, had waited too long before doing anything concrete about their relationship. They intended to get together, but they let their divorces drag on and on, haggling over terms and settlements. If pressed, they would insist it wasn't their fault: their former spouses were being difficult, another six months of therapy would be only fair, waiting a year would give the children time to adjust. But none of those things were the absolutes they claimed they were: a willingness to sit loose to them would have speeded up the process mightily.

Not that there was anything bad about doing the job prudently, right or fairly—if you could do so without putting off the future. But the time to work on a relationship is when it happens to you, not next year, or whenever Myrtle's lawyer thinks he's gotten her the best deal he can negotiate. Delay the job and you end up saying to your new partner the same thing you said to your old one: you matter to me, Melvin, but there are just these few other things that matter more, so let me take care of them first. You end up, in other words, having changed nothing. You're still trying to manage a major relationship without being willing to put the other person at the head of the line; and when the long-delayed future finally does drag itself onstage, you still won't have a clue why it differs so little from the past.

But the second part of the lesson was harder to put into practice. Even if two people were willing to stop being pikers and do whatever was necessary to fulfil the future of their relationship now, it was still easy for it to drop out of sight under the debris of daily living. Or, more accurately, to slip by slow degrees into being a merely future future again. For the remarried, the evils of the day are often more than sufficient: the usual problems of health, mood and temperament are multiplied by new ones with children, family, friends and money. The result is a present so depressing that the temptation to look to a better day is almost overwhelming. Life drifts back to being mostly when-and-if again: the only hopes are the off chances that Suzie will stop being a dropout, that his first wife will not be difficult, that her friends will end their standoff, that someday maybe there'll be enough money.

And in that frame of mind, it's hard not to come to the conclusion that the future, however much it was once invigoratingly present to their life, has simply evaporated again. Perhaps the most unnerving experience for the twice-married is the terrifying thought that maybe nothing has changed after all—that in spite of the expense of spirit and time, they have simply landed back in the old future-less present. And the only antidote for it is a daily effort to prove otherwise by deliberate acts that will impose the shape of the future on the present.

Madeleine wanted some specifics. I said I thought the first step was for the couple to be at each other's disposal— to be, as often as possible, servants to each other. After all, that was how it was with them when they first caught the glimpse of themselves as each other's future. If there was anything one of them could do for the other, it was done out of sheer delight at having a future in the present again. The trick was to keep that kind of mutual service going past the point of the initial enthusiasm for it. And it was worth mastering, because it was a two-way street: acts of service were sacraments, representations that also had the power to cause what they represented. You could do them because you already had the hope you were talking about; or you could do them without having it, and find it suddenly present. It was like a party: you might throw one as a result of a happiness already present; or, alternatively, you might banish unhappiness by throwing one. Either way, the believed future ended up here.

Therefore the simplest device for effecting that in a relationship was a settled habit of asking, "What can I do for you?"—or of thinking of it yourself and just doing it. And the reverse of that coin was not balking when you were asked to do something. People talked loosely about the desirability of "keeping in" or "putting back" the romance in a marriage; but if that ever worked out to more than just conjuring with emotions, it almost always meant a constant refreshing of the sense of surprise at being first in someone else's life. If that was indeed the future that was glimpsed, then every embodiment of it, no matter how small, would serve to renew the vision.

But beyond that, the other principal device was an equally studious habit of letting as many realizable futures as possible into each day to give it purpose. I brought up again the idea of working by jobs rather than by the clock. The benefit of that was that it made life into a sequence of purposeful acts instead of a mere endurance of the passage of time. Once again, the acts didn't have to be all that important. In fact, the unimportant ones—beds made, meals cooked, doors unstuck, closets cleaned—were almost better. There were more of them, and they were mercifully brief: the sense of purpose made up for its lack of greatness by arriving early and often.

The basic principle though was still the same: sacramental acts effect what they signify. They're not only results of a faith that's already here; they can also be causes of one that isn't. People often say they wish they could feel that the present is going somewhere; but because they concentrate more on the somewhere than the going, the experience eludes them. You can't steer a boat that's dead in the water; any direction will do for a start, just as long as it's believed in seriously enough to get us moving. Today, for example, my short-term, realizable futures include making bread and cooking you something oriental for supper. Even if the larger prospects of my life have a hard time breaking through to me, I will at least have let some purpose—and, therefore, motion—into my present. Fresh bread from the oven may not be the grand eschaton itself, but it works the same way. Getting there is more than half the fun: it's the whole secret of feeling human instead of dead.

IV

REMARRIAGE & DIVORCE

 Incidentally, that makes four jobs done so far without so much as a glance at the clock: one run to refresh the spirit, one omelet to fold into the system and, scrambled in with both of those, one leg up each on the subjects of illegitimacy and the future. Tuck into the eggs while I try to press our advantage.

We're on the subject of divorce as it relates to remarriage, and I want to keep it firmly in that context. Not just because it's already been worked to death as a topic in its own right, but because treating it in isolation is downright misleading. You can talk fruitfully about marriage as such because there are positive images that shed light on the institution. But divorce is not only full of negative images; it isn't even an institution. And, despite the occasional suggestion that we ought to dress it up as one by having a divorce ceremony analogous to the marriage rite, there's no way to change its nature. It's a sinking, not a launching. No amount of champagne can institutionalize shipwreck.

All genuine institutions have the ability to impose the shape of the future on the present. Whether you're involved in marriage or a nine-day Caribbean cruise, you're caught up in something whose purpose informs each new day and makes you glad to seize it. But not with divorce; just the opposite is true. Of itself, it installs no future; it simply abolishes one that presided over the past. If you're glad, it's because a bad trip has been canceled, not because you've been provided with a good one. The cancellation may have been necessary, or inevitable, or the best of a bad job, but as such it tells you nothing positive about what to do next—any more than being stopped in your tracks by a heart attack tells you, in and of itself, to take up jogging.

The reason, therefore, why I don't want to talk simply about divorce is that the subject helps no one. Like a coronary, a divorce incapacitates rather than enables. What it imposes on the present is not a hope out of the future but a fear out of the past. And however much anyone might be disposed to dwell on the details of its history— its rightness or wrongness, its fairness or unfairness, who was or was not to blame—it's all beside his present point. What he needs at that crucial juncture is either help to find a future to impose now, or encouragement in installing one he thinks he's found. The only reason for talking about a divorce at all is to prevent the carryover of it from botching up the installation.

As I said, we get all kinds of shipwrecked sailors through here. Some have been divorced without any immediate prospect of a new relationship; others come with a prospect in sight. But I don't find straight divorce talk useful in either case. The former mostly need to have their heads held and their wounds dressed—a ministry to which mulling over their divorces is about as helpful as picking at sores. As long as the quick of the past is exposed, no future, however lively, is likely to get through to them. And the latter group, even though they've gotten hold of a future, have just the same need to get off the dime of their past. It's nothing but a slug, I say; it can only jam any future they make the mistake of putting it in. For both types, therefore, what's needed is positive discouragement from dwelling on divorce. The subject is a loser; if we talk about it at all, my chief concern is to get them off it as quickly as possible.

It dies hard, though, so I've developed a way of classifying their comments to speed up the process. As far as I can see, there are only four things that can be said about a divorce, and only one of them has even an outside chance of being a useful beginning. I'll give you that one right now: It's to say that *I did it*, and to deal only with the strict consequences of that acceptance of responsibility. Since that's practically the last thing they're willing to say, however, we usually have to work our way through one or more of the other three denials.

The first way they mismanage the subject is to shift responsibility squarely onto somebody else's shoulders. They say, "*I* didn't do it." Their divorce was either the result of a spouse's behavior (described with varying degrees of charity or accuracy as nasty, cruel, sick or unhappy) or, if the speaker admits any hand in it at all, it was the work of someone no longer living in his skin: it was, he insists, a former "I" that did it—a sicker or more sinful person than the one who is now, thank God and/or therapy, able to sit up and take the nourishment of my scotch.

The second style of mismanagement is an ever-so-slight but nonetheless drastic revision of the first. They say, "I

didn't do *it*." Whatever it was that happened, it was not
the breakup of a marriage that they were involved in.
Either there was no marriage to begin with, or the one
that was there expired, or one of the parties to it ended
up morally dead; but in any case, by the time the day
came to do the nasty deed, there was nothing left to do it
to. The corpse had drowned before they shot it: therefore
they were innocent of murder. Like the first method of
exculpation, however, this leaves them with no way of
coping with the past as it actually was. If it still has access
to them in the present (and it does and will: while their
conscious mind pretends, they and others still remember),
that access is a one-way street. They can't get back to their
past. It becomes, and remains, an enigma.

That is why the third style of mismanagement is more
popular. People say, "Yes, I did it; but at least I didn't
do *that*." They admit a certain complicity in the undoing
of a marriage; but if they concede their guilt on the substance of the deed, they exculpate themselves on the
grounds of style. The devices they employ are numberless:
at least I didn't do it to a really nice guy, the way Sally
did; or commit adultery, like Martha, or be ungenerous
in the property settlement, like Irving; or be in such a
rush I refused counseling, like Morris; or manipulate the
children, or default on alimony, or hit the bottle—and so
on, if not into the sleep of conscience, at least into the
ethical twilight of the Pharisee's prayer: "My God, I thank
thee that I am not as other men are."

But however much those devices may be used, all three
of them are worse than useless. When a marriage has gone
sour, the only thing that will enable you to take its curse
off your present is forgiveness. Forgiveness of yourself and
forgiveness of everybody else concerned. The past was
whatever it was, and there is no way of going back to make
it different. And you did whatever you did: no amount of

subsequent exculpation can change a thing. The only thing such exercises achieve is to take your mind off what you really need: absolution.

If that sounds a little churchy, don't worry about it. In practice, the church is one of the chief encouragers of exculpation as a substitute for forgiveness, especially as far as marital failures are concerned. We shall have enough potshots to take at her to delight the heart of the most hardened sceptic. In any case, if the one agency we might have expected forgiveness from isn't making much of it, somebody—even a couple of strays in off the golf course—ought to have a go at it.

What's that? You rather thought it was time for a shower? Nonsense. We're just getting warmed up. Besides, who's watching the clock?

V

DIVORCE, INNOCENCE & GUILT

I hear a deeper objection forming in your mind, though. This talk about forgiveness makes you uneasy. "Are we," you ask me, "simply going to slip back into the old stigmatization of divorce as morally wrong? The subject is already riddled with blame. Isn't there some way to deal with it that's less guilt-producing than confession? Why can't people just concentrate on the good that comes of it and let it go at that?"

Let me answer you by making some distinctions. As far as your chariness about guilt and blame are concerned, I am with you at least part of the way. They do cripple people; and the act of confessing is indeed more likely to be an orgy of self-blame than a celebration of forgiveness. That may be because we have so seldom been forgiven that we have no confidence in the outcome; but whatever the reason, confession all too often looks like something positively bad for the soul.

But even though guilt is a loser, ignoring it is hardly the way to get rid of it. It's not as easy as it sounds to concentrate on the beneficial effects of divorce and let it go at that. For one thing, other people go right on holding us to blame, sometimes for years. For another, even if we manage to slough them off, we have ourselves to cope with. No matter what we do or don't do about our failures, the fact of them remains. Admission of responsibility, followed by forgiveness all around, seems to me the only realistic way of dealing with the fact.

That probably bothers you too, but I can't see any way around it. A divorce, no matter how many good or even holy results it produces, is always by nature a failure. It's the collapse of something that was meant to stand, a denial of what at least at one time seemed like a good idea. And no matter what we say to mitigate our complicity in the failure, there's no possibility of denying it altogether. Marriage, no matter how unadvisedly or lightly it's entered into, is always a joint venture. Consciously or not, each partner deeds to the other tremendous authority over his life. Even if they have no other fault than not exercising that power, it is a far-reaching fault indeed. For a man to say, for example, that it was his wife and not himself who ruined their marriage simply cannot be true. For as long as they were together, her actions were at least to some degree responses to his; if he did not make himself felt as a power in her life, he cannot fault her entirely. Her half-hearted commitment was at least partly the result of his half-throttle pursuit of their relationship.

Just to take the apparent male chauvinism off that, though, let me illustrate it with the sexes reversed. I knew a woman once whose marriage had broken up because of her husband's straying ways. That, at any rate, was how she saw it, even though he had been the one to ask for the divorce. In her own mind, she was a textbook case of the innocent party in adultery; like all such classic cases, however, her blamelessness did not make her conspicuously happy. I suggested to her that maybe it wasn't just because being a victim was no fun: the real trouble was she wasn't innocent.

She insisted she was: He was the one who had the affairs, and there was nothing she could have done to stop him. I disagreed. There were plenty of husbands not much different from hers who didn't wander. The reason they didn't was not moral superiority; it was because their wives, in no uncertain terms, had exercised power by staking a claim on them. How clearly, I asked, had she done that?

I knew the answer: not very. She started to defend her role as the patient, understanding wife, but I interrupted. Weren't there at least some others in her life to whom she told exactly what the limits of her tolerance were? Specifically, didn't she do that with her children? I knew they felt she did, so I pressed the comparison: she had power over her children and she used it; she had power over her husband and she didn't use it. For whatever reason, she gave them a ballast of expectation she held back from him. If he floated off, it was partly her doing.

And it didn't matter if her reasons were good or bad. If she was going to wait, in every circumstance of her life, for the moral quality of her actions to be unexceptionable, she would be forced, in some circumstances at least, to wait too long. In personal relationships, the overriding necessity was to give your partner your longest and strongest suit, no matter what it was. If all you had was anger, then you gave that. How he played it, of course, was his business; but if you held it back, he might as well have been playing on his own. Which, I added, might be a fair description of what he actually did.

She wondered, though: even supposing she had been

willing to let her anger out, what really could she have done about him? I said all she needed for that was a little imagination: she could have screamed, punched, bitten, wept or left—or, failing all those, she could have been the one who insisted on the divorce first. She asked what good that would have done. I said at least it would have made her a perpetrator rather than a victim—and given him a taste of her power in his life. She said it still might not have stopped him. Well, then, I said, you could have shot him: that slows down even the best of them.

She objected to my lack of moral seriousness. I didn't really mean it, did I, that people ought to do just anything that comes into their heads? I said that wasn't the question. The question was whether their fear of what they ought not to do would keep them from doing anything at all. If you made it your largest aim in life never to fail, you didn't thereby succeed; you simply deprived others— and yourself—of your possible contribution to success. Sure, I admitted, there were good reasons to think twice about pistols—and about fists, feet and snide remarks, too. But what I was concerned about was the root principle of her balking at all of them: she had laid on herself a necessity to be perfect. That sounds great until you realize how easily it converts into never having to need forgiveness. In some other world than this one, it might work; but all we've got here are sinners. Among us, sending the very best is not the first rule of relationships; once again it's caring enough to send what we have on hand and then, as necessary, begging pardon all around.

That meant pardon from yourself, too—after a suitable confession to whatever better self you may have thought you had: I am not now, nor have I ever been, a terrific person; but for these and all my other sins, I give myself pardon and absolution—just so I won't stop dead in my tracks and never get within a hundred miles of being any kind of person at all. Apply it to anything you like, I told her. Breadmaking or lovemaking, everything here fails to rise sometime. If you can't forgive yourself for having been no good at it, sooner or later you'll give it up entirely.

I think a little of that got through to her, but she went away still troubled by my apparently loose views on morality. Somehow, I always strike my hearers as being on the opposite side of whatever their favorite moral position may be: if she found me too freewheeling, you were afraid I was going to slip back into calling divorce a wrong. I'm in good company, though. Saint Paul offended both Jews and Greeks: the former with lectures on the futility of trying to justify themselves by the law and the latter with guilt trips because they didn't keep it. And his point was the same as mine: we all fall short of what we are obliged to be; therefore, forgiveness is the only thing that can keep our relationships going. Forgiveness, not exculpation. If we take ourselves off the hook by denying the shortfall or by fudging the obligation, we simply make forgiveness inconceivable. Both have to be faced. Hence the appearance, in Saint Paul and in me, of talking out of two sides of the mouth.

If that makes me sound illegitimate all around, so be it. I think it also might just make us free enough to find a fresh grip on the subject.

VI

EX ME NO EXES

Let me shift the illustration slightly to show you what I mean.

Most of the divorced persons who come through here are either remarried or in the throes of getting themselves that way. And, predictably, they have the habit of referring to the partners of their previous marriages as their ex-wives or ex-husbands. To them, the usage seems not only convenient but somehow morally necessary: without it, they can't feel free to do what they're doing. Nevertheless, I challenge them on it.

What's wrong, I ask them, with owning up to the fact that they have two spouses? After all, when they took them, they did so in a ceremony which more than likely insisted they were doing so for life. Is any useful purpose served by reneging on that idea just because they were not up to following it through? Isn't the whole notion of "exes" a form of moral bookkeeping that is suspect in almost any other context?

For it's only in connection with divorce that we use it as if it made sense. No matter how badly my relationships go, for example, with my sister, I would not think of talking seriously about her as my ex-sister. And if children are sometimes inveigled into thinking of their mother's ex-husband as their ex-father, we almost always recognize that as a kind of emotional dirty pool. Most significantly, even when the marriage relationship suffers its most permanent disruption—in widowhood—we don't talk about ex-wives or ex-husbands. First wives, maybe, or former husbands; but the phrase is used only for clarity's sake.

So, I ask them, why the prevalence of exes among the divorced? If a remarried widow can admit that two men have been her husband, why can't her friend, the divorcée? The answer, of course, is that the prefix is being used not simply to identify a partner in a previous relationship, but to deny the relationship. But why, I want them to tell me, should that be?

At that point, they usually try to pass the buck: it all goes back, they insist, to the old ecclesiastical doctrine that only death could absolve you from the exclusivity of the marriage vow. The divorced, even in these enlightened times, still feel the pressure of that and, lacking the death of a partner to set them free, they supply themselves with the death of the role.

I, however, decline the pass. I tell them that I both agree and disagree with the church. I think she has made the mistake of trying to maintain a contradiction. On the one hand, she has proclaimed that marriage is indissoluble. As far as I can see, that's true—and not only of marriages. All my relationships, to the extent that they have even a minute's duration, enter irreversibly into my history. It makes no sense to deal with their shipwrecks by inventing devices to prove that history never happened.

But on the other hand, that is just what the church did;

at least for a good many centuries. She encouraged people to deal with marital failure by denying the marriage instead of admitting the failure. Annulment—the dissolving of the professedly indissoluble by legal fiction—was her standard device for making remarriages morally acceptable. How, I ask them, do they think she got herself mired in such a blatantly unrealistic and obviously contradictory business?

If they demur and try to defend annulments, I object. Admittedly, there is a kind of logic to them in theory; but in practice it simply doesn't apply. If you could find a pure case of shotgun wedding (a couple forced together on the basis of no joint history at all), obviously you would have a convincing case of duress. But even more obviously you would have a case of no relationship. Shotguns, however, were never loaded over such nonprovocation. There was always, and often literally, something there.

And if they object that that wasn't necessarily the best kind of relationship—that all the annulment system did was provide a way out of mistakes—I make a distinction: yes, people do need a way out of certain relationships; but wouldn't it be better to provide it by simply accepting their admission of the mistake? Didn't that make more sense than the strange insistence that if you couldn't, or wouldn't finish something you started, your only hope was to prove you hadn't started it?

Which brings us, of course, to the point. Ex-husbands, ex-wives and ex-marriages all have one common denominator in the minds of those who pronounce them so: the usage is a deliberate substitution of exculpation for forgiveness. Where ordinary mortals get that preference from is fairly obvious. From childhood on, all of us would rather proclaim our innocence than our guilt. But how the church acquired a preference for ex-marriages over failed ones is harder to understand.

After all, she is by profession sent to proclaim forgiveness to sinners. By the strict logic of her mission—and by the example of a Lord who was a friend of tax farmers and call girls—you would no more expect her to be finicky about dealing with moral failures than you would a carpenter to be chary of dealing with wood. And yet she is. In spite of the number and frequency of preachers' utterances about sin, the main idea they convey is that it's more important to avoid being bad than to admit it. Being good, not being forgiven, is presented as the touchstone of the godly life.

As a result, the church has gotten itself into some positions that are strange indeed. Take the notion of vows: marriage vows, priestly vows, whatever. On the face of it, there is nothing wrong with making a solemn promise to commit yourself to something; in fact, to be unwilling to do so is usually a sign that nothing much is actually being proposed. But on the reverse of it, there is also nothing wrong with anticipating a fair amount of welshing on such promises. Yet what the church has often done in practice is to treat the breaking of vows not simply as a sin to be dealt with in the fellowship of forgiven sinners, but as grounds for expulsion from that fellowship.

If that charge seems to you to be less true than it once was, don't be too quick to conclude it's false. Admittedly, some churches have renounced excommunicating run-of-the-mill members because they remarry after divorce; but even among them, it is still common to find divorced and remarried clergy dealt with by ostracism rather than forgiveness. And, in the churches that have not renounced excommunication, there are discomfiting signs that they will, if anything, use it more rather than less. The recent return in the Roman Church to the hard line of refusing laicization to priests who have broken their vow of celibacy is not likely to encourage anybody to see the church as a haven for sinners.

As I said, such chariness about sin in an institution dedicated to removing the burden of it is hard to understand. But the result is clear enough: the word gets out that innocence, even at the price of denying facts, is preferable to forgiveness, even if it's free. Unfairly, perhaps, I've laid this at the door of the church, because that's where the attitude originated. But by now, the chariness is so firmly entrenched in even the secular attitudes toward divorce and remarriage that the churches could purge themselves of it tomorrow, and your sister-in-law, your best friends or your neighbors up the street would go right on exing every failure in your life—and encouraging you to do the same.

All my guests, therefore, are urged to admit to as many wives or husbands as they have actually had—and to consider that, in varying circumstances, they still have them all right now. If that threatens to make a mess of the moral bookkeeping they've so far been devoted to, I suggest only that it takes less emotional and historical fudging and could, accordingly, be closer to the truth.

At least that way, I tell them, nobody has to get the ex.

VII

MONOGAMY, POLYGAMY & ROMANCE

 I remember once making that same argument when a fairly conservative friend was in the room. He had a sociological turn of mind, and he took off from my comments into a disquisition on the idea that serial polygamy has replaced monogamy as the form of marriage most common among us: we don't actually countenance having several spouses at once, he said; but as long as people have them in succession, we don't object. He suggested that my insistence on "no exes" seemed to be a capitulation to the general collapse of standards, and that I—and the church too, for that matter—would do better to go back to defending life-long exclusive monogamy as the ideal.

The trouble with arguments of that sort is that they proceed mostly by throwing slogans at reality. Their net effect is that the facts of the situation go unexamined. When confronted with them, my response is not simply to disagree, but to make all the distinctions I can in the hope of getting past the name-calling. The method involves a good deal of both affirmation and denial—much of it apparently perverse. I will concede points that I'm expected to fight and defend things I might otherwise attack, just to open up the subject. To me, this seems nicely Socratic, but when I tried to justify it to my friend, he objected: I wasn't playing Socrates; I was just being a nudge. I answered him with an example of the method. Yes, I was being a nudge, but what did he think Socrates sounded like?

Anyway, my first riposte was to the charge of countenancing serial polygamy. To me, the phrase is one of those resounding stigmatizations that make a loud noise against the target without coming anywhere near the bull's-eye. To begin with, polygamy of all sorts, serial or not, has a long history. The idea that it's an unqualified evil, and therefore that every manifestation of it is simply to be condemned, just won't hold up. There was a fair amount of it in the Old Testament; and if it was later abandoned in favor of monogamy, it was never—even in the extreme form of royal concubinage—seriously tut-tutted over by moralists. They simply invented justifying exceptions for it (the need, for example, of Jacob to get the twelve tribes off to a flying start), and got on with the story.

And in the new dispensation, the same thing was done. Admittedly, the device by which it was accomplished (namely, annulment) paid homage to monogamy in principle—and its application was limited to the high and mighty; but in practice, the result was hardly different from the so-called serial polygamy that exists among us now.

More important, the morality of it was in fact upheld. What matters most in questions of morals is not the particular argument by which certain conduct is justified, but whether or not morally serious people actually end up justifying it. The arguments, after all, proceed from premises which are themselves not only debatable, but which seldom get the debate they deserve.

Take the history of the nineteenth century missionary movement. On the basis of the received matrimonial standards, Christian proselytizers, when they addressed themselves to societies in which polygamy was practiced, commonly insisted that converts get rid of all wives but one. On a different moral premise, however—say, one that put first and foremost the obligation of a man not to deprive others of their status in society—they could just as well have gone along with the institution. The casting off of surplus wives was hardly a universal good. The women thus disposed of became, in fact, outcasts; an ethic of respect for persons would have taken that into account.

What is at issue between polygamy and monogamy is not immorality or morality, but two different, equally "moral" institutions. Had the missionaries been as resourceful in making compromises as the biblical commentators had been, perhaps weightier moral issues might have had a chance to come to the fore. In that light, I would be willing to concede the charge that America is now to a large degree a serially polygamous society and claim that what is needed is for the church to deal with it as a missionary situation—and in a better way than she did in the last century. For the same reasons: the moral damage done by encouraging people to think their previous marriages must somehow be dissolved is greater than any harm that could come from insisting on some kind of continuing relationship.

That, of course, always raises hackles. "Are we simply," people ask, "to forget about monogamy? Just because there are unfortunate effects from resisting polygamy doesn't mean it's an equally good moral system. Doesn't the church

—or anyone else, in fact—have an obligation to uphold the best?"

At that point, I make some more distinctions. Yes, monogamy is undoubtedly a better system, at least in principle. It calls for the fullest, least divided commitment of person to person and therefore comes closest to being a diagram of the deepest meaning of love. And yes, there's even reason to beat the drum for the best. However, that's not what's at issue. I may have accepted the charge that we're a polygamous society a few minutes ago, but now I have to deny it. The many marriages we currently make are all, in intention, resolutely monogamous. Indeed, the reason for the succession of matrimonial relationships is precisely our commitment to the idea that there can only be one. Successive monogamy, not serial polygamy, is what people actually have in mind.

In fact, monogamous exclusivity is so firmly entrenched among us that it has more need of critics than defenders. Not that it still isn't the best notion of marriage. It is; but it's already buttressed to a fare-thee-well. And the reason for that is that it has for several centuries ridden piggyback on another institution which is even more uncritically accepted: romantic love as the sovereign basis for matrimonial relationships.

That supremacy was not entirely a logical development: romantic love had its beginnings in resolutely extramarital alliances like those of Lancelot and Guinevere. On its face, it would seem an unlikely and undependable candidate to replace parental choice as the method for selecting marriage partners. And indeed, it was only long after its first appearance in the high middle ages that it assumed its present role. But whatever its shortcomings (as a notoriously repeatable way of choosing bedfellows, it makes a poor foundation for a supposedly unrepeatable one; as the most tyrannical experience of all, it threatens constantly to disallow all other pretenders), it does have one characteristic that suits marriage to a tee. No matter how often it recurs, it is always forever. People who believe their love affairs will last till the stars fall have little difficulty making promises that last only till death do them part.

Despite all the pop sociology, therefore, it is precisely plain old monogamy—not serial polygamy or any other revised version of the institution—that most of us still believe in. To be sure, from time to time people come along who think they have a better idea: open marriage, sexual liberation or whatever; but since it's not our notions but our faith that's the engine of our commitments, it's our beliefs, not our ideas that carry the day. As long as those don't change, the institution that holds out for them will need neither defense nor membership drives.

Accordingly, it's the people involved in the institution— the furry bodies who insist on making the grand promises and believing in the monumental designs—who need the most help. But as obvious as that might seem, the truth is they are practically the last ones to get it. Strangely, and dangerously, we defend marriage more readily than the people in it, in spite of the fact that they alone share flesh and blood with us. Why that should be, though—why we should prefer the company of an alien to that of our own kind—takes a little more explaining.

Enter here, therefore, my theory of marriage as an angel.

VIII

MARRIAGE, THE ANGELS & SUCCESS

The first thing to be said is that marriage isn't the only alien to which we give power over our lives. In the widest sense, all institutions are nonhuman. The most visible of them—school, state, family, corporation—may seem to be just groupings of people, but in fact they have a life not only separable from the lives of their members, but fundamentally different. And the less visible ones—the ones which, like fatherhood, motherhood, romance and marriage, look principally like concepts or roles—have the same deep incompatibility with human nature. However gladly or often we invite them to preside over our lives, we remain, at the roots of our being, not their cup of tea.

Think, for example, of a school. On its face, it looks like nothing more than a collection of ordinary mortals dedicated to a merely human end: the enhancement of individuals by the communication of knowledge and skill.

As everyone knows, however, no school can commit itself unqualifiedly to that end. It will tolerate the presence of particular individuals only if they are willing and able to play by a set of rules that are always imminently at odds with their humanity. Specifically, they can stay in the institution only as long as they don't do something that human beings have always done with great regularity: fail.

I was once asked, at a conference I chaired at a church-related school, to give some (presumably favorable) comments about the role of the "Christian" school. I responded by saying I didn't think there could be any such thing. There could be good schools or bad schools, and there could be schools run by Christians or by others; but the school itself, as an institution, could never tolerate the violation of its nature that would be entailed by being Christian. I was asked what I meant. I asked back: How many courses could a student fail and be kept in the fellowship? Seven? Seventy times seven?

The question was obviously a paraphrase of Jesus' dialogue with Peter about how often he should forgive his brother. My questioner's answer to it was to make a distinction: A certain amount of absolution was permissible in a school—the faculty at hand, in fact, had just lowered the passing grade—but unlimited tolerance of failure was not possible; the school had its standards to think of. I asked: Why? He answered: It would go out of business if it didn't. I asked again: What was so bad about that? Wasn't the greatest act of love described by Jesus as the laying down of one's life for one's friends? Hadn't my questioner just proved my point for me? Namely, that by the most fundamental necessity of its nature, a school was incapable of being either a brother or a friend to anybody— at least not in the limitless sense that the adjective "Christian" would require.

It was at that point that I invented the notion of the institution as angel. When the old theologians discoursed about angels—about the Cherubim, Seraphim and Thrones, about Dominions, Principalities and Powers—they assigned to those exalted creatures certain notable attributes. I am not at all concerned here as to whether in fact there are such beings. The fathers, of course, thought there were: their world was a vast tissue of remarkable creatures, some below us on the ladder of creation, some above. But I shall pass that question, because whether or not there are real, old-fashioned angels "up there," there are plenty of current entities that look and act a great deal like them right down here.

Angels, in the old theology, were rational, incorporeal creatures. Their knowledge, by definition, was perfect; and their being—because they had no bodies subject to decay—was immortal. They might, to be sure, be put out of existence by God, but short of that, there was no way in which they could ever voluntarily entertain the prospect themselves.

Behold, therefore, the Institution as we know and love it—to our own often endless discomfort. Take any one you like: Church, State, School, the Kennedys, the Kowalskis, the Loyal Order of Moose or IBM. All of them, according to their rational natures, are pure and perfect; and not a single one of them can ever think of putting itself out of business. The U.S.A., for example, will no doubt go the way of all flesh someday, just as Egypt, Rome, the Spanish monarchy and the British Empire did. But it is simply inconceivable that it will happen by the vote of both houses of Congress.

Or, to change the illustration slightly, think of the Presidency. Individual human beings may occupy it; and, as flesh and blood, they will all go just as certainly as they came. But in their institutional role as Presidents, there is just no way that they will ever abolish the Presidency.

They might violate it, but all that happens then is that it abolishes them. The thing is an angel. At whatever cost to anybody else, it simply has to live.

Interestingly, it is just that fact—now made so painfully clear by the history of the twentieth century—that led modern theologians to do a kind of perverse end run around the question of angels. Seventy, even fifty years ago, hardly anyone could find a use for the topic. But in the face of the rise of Communism, Fascism, Multinational Corporationism or whatever else you care to name, they rediscovered the idea of the demonic. The evils of the world simply could not be accounted for by blaming them on the flaws, however numerous, of human nature. The only reasonable explanation was to lay them at the door of those flaws insofar as they were enlisted *in the service of some other "entity"* that in the last analysis was not playing a human game at all.

When Michael the Archangel had his heavenly confrontation with Satan (or Satan with Michael—they both saw themselves as right), the only possible outcome was War in Heaven. The question of one pardoning the other never came up—and the idea of one laying down his life for the other remained as inconceivable as ever. The fact that one was right and the other wrong made no difference at all to what happened. Angel or demon, the only method either had of dealing with rebellion, failure, illegitimacy or even difference was war.

And so too here on earth, where (to our great delight and unavoidable peril) we make common cause with angelic entities. Note both elements in that parenthesis. The angels that surround us—even the demonic ones—are beautiful in our eyes. That is precisely the root of their power. In that light, Anti-Semitism and Holy Matrimony are both of them compelling visions. If the first is wicked and the second good, it takes nothing off its ability to enlist the beauty-smitten in its service. But that service remains, in either case, a matter of consorting with an alien. Given its own definition of "the good," neither of them can tolerate derelictions in its servitors. Hence the peril of having any truck with them at all.

And the danger is, if anything, greater in the case of the ones that happen to be "right." With wicked angelic designs, there is always the hope that we will break with them when we see the light. But when the true brightness is chosen and we fail *that*—ah, then we have nothing left but a bind. Its charm will not let us go, but its nature cannot keep us on. We have become illegitimate in a league that has no room for illegitimacy. Hence, once again, my enthusiasm for the league of outcasts in which all divorced and remarried persons find themselves—and my constant nagging of them not to give up their membership in a hurry. It's the only company in which they have even a chance of catching sight of their own faces again.

For what the angels do to failures is simply say they never knew them. Therefore there is no possibility of anyone's recovering the vision of himself as a working human being as long as he remains in a context that makes a passing grade the supreme test. In spite of the fact that people always try to do it, I discourage them whenever I can. There's just no point in trying to work your history around so that it can be seen as right. In the first place, there will, as I said, almost always be some others who won't concede the point. In the second, there is no way in which the offended Institution of Matrimony can be talked into giving you a medal. And in the last, you can't honestly even pin one on yourself. At the bottom of the pile of justifications, there is always the knowledge of just what hand you had in whatever happened.

The only way the divorced and remarried could shake

the entail of their love affair with the Angel of Marriage would be to renounce marrying altogether. But since they haven't done that, the best thing to do is to admit such guilt as they have and get on with the one piece of business the angels can never understand: standing wrong but forgiven in your own skin.

I have come around once again, you see, to my pet subject. In a way, I wish I could promise you I was through with it, but I can't. We talk endlessly about finding our identity, but most of the time all that means is cooking up one that some angel or other will approve of. And it overlooks completely the fact that we already have an identity available just for the admitting of it. Forgiveness is the only way back to the only face we have.

What I can promise you, however, is that I will now stop this more or less high-flown patter and let the day proceed. Go take your shower while I start the bread. When you come back, I'll be down, if not to earth, at least to the kneading board.

The angels, I dare say, don't understand that either.

IX

SUCCESS, FAILURE &
FORGIVENESS

Ah, you're back.

The bread is well along. I'm at the point of needing no more flour on the board, so from here on out it's just a matter of kneading energetically till I get the texture I want.

How long? Well, we've been through that wicket once already. Clock time is not the best guide for human operations. If I were a kneading machine, you would probably set me for seven minutes; but since people run with such differing speeds and powers, the only real answer is: till the hand and the eye tell you you're done. If someone presses me for a specific length of time, however, I'm not totally stubborn about it. I size up his personality and, if I see a fair amount of vigor and resolve, I tell him: twice as long as you think. If I see next to none, I tell him: four times. Forced to the wall for an answer, I say fifteen minutes; but then I invite him to watch. Experience is the only real teacher.

As with life, there are hundreds of variables which, if you considered all their permutations and combinations, would only depress you with the thousands of disasters possible in the process. No instructor—unless the angels have talked him into running a school—should try to give foolproof instructions. What people most need is the lesson that it's perfectly all right to suffer your own foolishness gladly—to fail, as you often will, but not to let that stop you. It's your bread, or your life, that you're after. The biggest single obstacle you can put in the way of achieving it is to make success at it the first consideration.

But I said I wouldn't dwell on that any more for now, so I won't. Besides, it wasn't what I had in mind while I was kneading. Actually, I was thinking about my first, or previous (but not ex-) wife. We learned to cook together and, over twenty-seven years of marriage, formed each other's tastes and skills. It was, in fact, one of the best things we did. Even now, three years into a second marriage, I find myself wanting to show her the results of something I've worked on, or to call her up and ask just how she made a dish that, for the first time, I'm finally making all by myself. In those moods, she is not even previous or former; she's just the wife I am, strangely, not cooking for or with at the moment.

That's not nostalgia. By some defect of character or missing piece of equipment, I have never suffered from more than the slightest twinge of it. And it's not sadness either. It's just that I see no way of successfully denying the lifelongness of any marriage. So when the mood hits me—or Madeleine, for that matter—we feel free to drop all the fuss over who came first or last. What's the point of denying our prior spouses, either to each other or to the world? I, for one, did more than my share of that in the past; why should I keep up such a dangerous habit now?

Divorce, no matter how much it looks like a monumental denial of another person, doesn't have to be seen that way at all. To be sure, it comes at the end of a whole series of denials within a relationship—and it occurs precisely when, for one reason or another, those denials finally get out of hand. But to think that continuation of the denial is the way to get one's relationships, present or past, back in hand is silly. What people need from us— and what we need to see ourselves as giving them—is affirmation. Even if they don't think they need it at all. The most important love letters have to be written without the encouragement of a warm welcome.

You gather from that, I suppose, that our enthusiasm here for affirming former partners is not exactly shared by them. If so, you gather correctly. All divorces are different. Some start in acrimony and proceed to detente; others, like Madeleine's and mine, begin with mutual agreement and run downhill from there. If I had to be as accurate as possible right now, I would say that our mates are near the bottom of the affirmation slide as far as we are concerned—with one or the other of them perhaps, or perhaps not, on the way up. But that's their privilege and problem. If it's understandable—and it is: we were the ones who brought the divorces to a head—it still doesn't make denial a good idea. Marriages are lifelong for the simple reason that we are, too. No matter what shape they're in, the sooner they're patched as much as possible, the better the rest of life's length.

You are curious, though. If we're so given to affirmation, how come we didn't try that in our first marriages, instead of compounding the difficulty by starting a second? Well, I shouldn't speak for Madeleine, so I won't. For myself, all I can say is that I was never aware of my biggest denial of my first wife until I had already made a fatal affirmation of my second. I was a world-class builder of compartments inside my own head. Because I was involved with a number of people—and because I felt I could not affirm certain of them without denying others —I took to the device of keeping them scrupulously separate in my mind. That worked pretty well, considering, but it had two serious drawbacks.

The first was that it got me into the Billy Sol Estes syndrome: one shining purpose and two—or three, or four or more—sets of books. You can keep that sort of thing going only as long as you are clever, lucky and don't lose your gusto for a lifetime career of fudging books. But the other difficulty is that even if you manage all of it, the other people in your life, no matter how kindly disposed, begin to notice the compartments you've put them in. And they do so simply because they find there are more and more parts of your life from which they are excluded. You—the whole you, that is, the plain old single lump of humanity in front of them—have less and less to say. In the end, your topics get down pretty close to the weather and the checkbook.

What Madeleine did for and to me (the "for" is what it was, but the "to" is what it felt like) was to teach me, for the first time in maybe forty years, how to talk. And she did it by the shattering expedient of not letting me get away with even a single silence. If I ever knew how ordinary people communicated, I had clean forgotten it for most of my adult life. I would watch two men in a bar or two women in a supermarket and be totally amazed at the fact that they always had something to say. "How," I asked Madeleine, "do they do that?" "It's simple," she said. "People—especially people like you—are always *thinking* something; all they have to do is open their mouths and let it come out. It's called *conversation*, I think. Would you like to try it?"

For someone whose first thought was always whether x

could be said to y—and whose second thought was usually not to say it—that was about as natural as breathing under water. I did try it, though, and once I got the knack of kicking through the compartments, there was no stopping. I told her all, and somewhat more than all, that anyone ever needed to know about me. That liberation, coupled with certain other resident attractions in the lady herself, led me to the point where, on one open-mouthed afternoon, I heard the words, "I'm not walking away from you," come out of my mouth. I was not aware of having thought such an unthinkable thing, but having said it, it suddenly seemed neither unthinkable nor undoable. And so we did.

So now, if you ask me again why I didn't take my new-found talent home and try it out on my first wife, my answer is simply that I chose not to. I will not say I chose rightly. There are too many different views of what constitutes rightness in such a situation. I will only say that, as I saw it, and still see it, all the choices open to me (go home, go to Madeleine, go get lost) involved failing somebody. I was in the position of the suddenly awakened driver of a car speeding toward a crowd of people: the decision was not whether to hit anyone; only whom. The situation confers a kind of dreadful liberty. But since I was the one who was going to do the damage in any case, I figured I might as well make the choice my own.

If you want to lecture me about the lack of niceness in that, go ahead. Hand me the transcript and I'll sign it sight unseen. And if you want to tell me that I should have been a more careful driver, I'll sign up for driver's school too: I have no interest in being in that predicament ever again. Telling my wife that I was leaving her to marry someone else was the single worst thing I have ever done to another human being in under thirty minutes. Other bad jobs took longer and did more damage maybe, but that one won the prize for succinctness. If it was not the last time in my life I tried to see myself as a good guy, it was the first time I knew the attempt was never going to work. Since then, I have given up accepting invitations to justify myself: I'm still wrong often enough now; so what good would it do me to cook up some proof that I was right then? Better I should learn to admit failure. That way, at least I have nowhere to go but up.

X

REMARRIAGE &
CLEAN HANDS

Thousand and one, thousand and two, thousand and three . . .

What am I doing? Just hold on for a few seconds . . . thousand and eight, thousand and nine, thousand and off!

Pardon my rudeness, but I don't dare distract myself while I'm giving the oven a short shot of heat to bring it up to eighty-five or ninety degrees. It's too easy to forget and overheat things. If it's done right, though, the warmth, plus the soggy towel I put under the bowl, turns it into a perfect proof box for the rising of the dough. All you do is repeat the count from time to time during the process, especially after the final shaping. Homemade bread doesn't have to be heavy. If a lot of it has the heft of a doorstop, it's only because most people underproof their loaves. But even for that, you can't set a time. Two hours is a rough rule for the last rising before baking, but if you've got the dough in a coolish place, it can take longer. Bread—and everything else—proceeds at its own pace, not ours.

There are, of course, theoretical considerations in all processes; if you had full knowledge and control of the variables, you could decide how and when to act by reason alone. But we seldom know enough. In life as it's actually lived, we move mostly by guesswork out of experience; the best we can hope for from theory is that it will help us understand, after the fact, what we did wrong.

All of which leads me to think that this is as good a place as any to talk about something that came up in passing while I was reminiscing about my first marriage: the sub- ject of "clean" versus "dirty" divorces. In spite of the fact that all divorces are obviously failures to honor promises we once had every intention of keeping, society as a whole has not yet completed the transition it set out to make in its attitude toward them. In the old days, all such failures were simply condemned: if people broke up lawful mar- riages, they were considered outside the pale. No matter that the reasons might have been understandable: the deed itself could not be absolved.

We have largely abandoned that view now, but the habit of condemnation dies more slowly. And not just because of human cussedness. Remarriage, especially after divorce, is a dangerous if fascinating phenomenon for a society to allow. Few marriages are so perfect that the possibility— maybe even the desirable possibility—of breakup has not occurred to the partners involved. To them, the spectacle of people who have actually broken up, and who never- theless are accepted by the community, is a threat, or a challenge or both.

Hence our tendency, even when we try to deal in a new, more enlightened way with divorce, still to balk at dealing with the phenomenon itself. We will approve of remar- riages, but not as such; whenever we can, we prefer to handle them under the moral species of the hardship case. Poor Martha, for example—who lived with that impossible chauvinist, George, and tried so hard to make it work, and stuck it out so many years, and lost her health and her youth and her looks, and finally almost broke down completely—poor old Martha has every right to find happiness with a wealthy and titled Englishman whose wife, God rest her soul, died of some loathsome disease. But bring on thirty-one-year-old Jennifer at 118 pounds in a red one-piece bathing suit and let her carry on a flaming affair with the lawyer she eventually marries—while reliable Fred, her long-suffering husband, sits home nights taking care of the children she never really cared about, you know—and see what happens. If she has any friends at all when she's done, you can be sure they'll be new ones.

Society, you see, has not really gotten itself to the point of being able to ask Martha or Jennifer or George or Fred what they themselves want to do. Or, better said, it still can't bring itself to sit still for the answers they might give. That's not to say that any of their responses are necessarily going to be truthful, edifying or even entertaining. Only that they're theirs, and that that's practically the last thing we're willing to take into consideration. We are, as it were, halfway to accepting the proposition that people ought to be allowed to run their lives with their own hands, but we won't have gotten all the way until we can stop judging them by whether or not their hands were clean.

I was involved, not too many years ago, in the rewriting of the Episcopal Church's marriage laws. (I have since, of course, been accused of writing my own ticket, but that isn't true: in the first place, the idea of my ever getting a divorce was a million miles from my mind in those days; and in the second, when I actually did apply for a ticket, the authorities figured out a way of saying I couldn't have one.) Nevertheless, the so-called liberalized laws were overwhelmingly passed, and they were based squarely on many of the principles I've been carrying on about: people are the only ultimate authorities on their own choices; sin, failure and stupidity don't stop God from dealing with us, so they shouldn't stop the church; annulments and other legal fictions are no help in leading a real life. It looked for all the world as if a better day was coming.

However, when that revision was passed along to the local authorities of the church for administration, there was considerable slippage from the principles. They felt deeply uncomfortable with the idea of taking anyone's word about anything—even if it was as close to the person's bone as his marriage. So, even though all the old canonical flimflam was gone—even though the church, on her books, no longer insisted on proving that all your marriages except the current one were invalid—new moral and psychological flimflam was invented on the spot. If you could prove you were once bad or sick but had, before you remarried, gotten good and healthy, you could be accepted and approved. But if you would not admit you were sick, or if you insisted on remarrying while you were still a sinner, it was no go. You were scandalizing the troops.

That, of course, was an odd line for an organization dedicated to proclaiming the scandalous gospel that God died for us while we were yet sinners; but when you think about it, it's understandable enough. Human beings have always preferred being right to being forgiven, and since the church on earth is composed of nothing but, it always had a hard time keeping the offer of forgiveness from being buried under the insistence of goodness. Because, when the church worries about the scandal of seeming to countenance bad behavior, it suffers from two things: one, an excessive timorousness on the part of the clergy (a timorousness which tends to increase as they ascend in the hierarchy); and two, a lay preoccupation with scandal which has been produced by the failure of the clergy to put the gospel of forgiveness first. The chickens of hundreds of years of Law instead of Grace come home to roost: the good news, if it's preached at all, sounds dangerously bad; and the bad news that only the righteous can be saved becomes what everyone wants to hear.

How the church got into that bind is a long story, but one feature of it seems worth illustrating. For centuries, the church had rightly seen that it could not honestly claim to care much for men's souls if it did not likewise care for their bodies: it therefore went, quite literally, into the hospital business. But when the modern world, again rightly, decided that men's minds could be as sick as their bodies—and that therapy could therefore be psychological as well as physiological—the church was caught off guard.

Back in the days when it was simply fighting physical disease, its fundamental message about human life was not seriously jeopardized: people, even cured people, never forgot they would all someday die. And the church never let them. She nursed them back to health with one hand and taught the resurrection of the dead with the other. No problem.

But when the notion of mental sickness came along, she was tempted to hope for rather more than she should have from therapy. With bodily sickness, she never took the view that recovery in any way absolved either her or her children from having to face the body's major theological and, indeed, ontological problem: death. But when it came to helping them get their heads together, she unwarrantably began to hope that mankind's other major problem—sin—could somehow be abolished by treatment.

Stated baldly like that, it's not only an exaggeration but a falsehood. But the trick was, it was never stated baldly.

What happened was that in practice—one instance at a time, and in more and more instances as the twentieth century rolled on—she found herself saying of those who were off life's mark: they must be sick. But there is a trap in that. You start, in apparent kindness, by saying someone is not so much a sinner as he is unwell. Then, in even more kindness, you offer to send him for treatment. With that, however, you have come very near to closing the door on the gospel. Because if he gets well, you find yourself taking him back principally on the grounds that he is no longer off the mark; and if he does not, you are tempted to despair of him because he is incurable; but in no case do you leave yourself—nor does the church leave herself— much room to take him back according to your original charter: as a forgiven sinner, with guarantees only of your perpetual forgiveness, and no questions asked about the depth, duration or even existence of his reform.

When the Prodigal Son was in the far country eating hog slop, he made a number of decisions: that he had sinned against God, that he was no longer worthy to be his father's son, and that he would go home, explain all that and ask for a job as a hired hand. On the strength of those, he got up and went. The first thing his father did, however, before the boy got even one word out of his mouth, was to run tearing down the road and smother him with kisses. The second thing he did was listen to his confession—from which, after all that kissing, the boy sensibly removed the part about coming home to be a flunky. He was a son. A rotten son, but a son. And he was there. The third thing his father did was throw him the biggest party they ever had.

Do you see? All the old man really asked his son was: "What do you want to do with who you are? I gave you the money to do everything you've done so far, even if it was stupid; and I'm giving you forgiveness so you can do everything you're going to do from here on out—even if it turns out to be dumb too. It's your life. You're my son. We're both stuck. Let's go in and have a drink."

Sounds good, doesn't it? Too bad it's the hardest thing in the world for anybody to do.

XI

REMARRIAGE &
THE FEAR OF MISTAKES

 The guardians of society, however, whether official or self-appointed, are rarely willing to let the moral bookkeeping go at that. They find it insufficient simply to say that it's hard to accept someone's word about what he wants to do with his life. They feel compelled to compound the difficulties by attaching a list of attendant dangers to the proposition. As a result, prudence rather than acceptance becomes their main business.

Were they to have dealt with the returning Prodigal, for example, they would first have tried to be sure he was coming home for good reasons. Unlike the father in the parable, they would not have rushed into kissing; they would have waited till they were sure he wasn't just making a pit stop for clean clothes, a free lunch or more cash. And even if they satisfied themselves that he honestly intended to repent, they would worry about the possibility of self-deception on his part. Sure, he feels like coming home now, they would say, but what about two months hence? Wouldn't we do better to hold off the party until he's had some counseling? How can we know at this point that it's not all a mistake?

Indeed, so deep is our habit of minimizing risk before we extend acceptance that we say such things to ourselves, even if the guardians don't. I once had a conversation with an often-married friend who had yet another marriage—to the woman, in fact, who was sitting with him on my couch—rather vaguely in prospect. It was obvious, after just thirty minutes, that vagueness, not marriage, was his major problem: not only was the lady in question being pursued in a dither of half-heartedness and one-handedness; all his previous wives—and practically everything else in his life—had been pursued in the same way. I suggested that, for once, he should just go ahead and do what he had in mind—but do it, for a change, with both hands.

He worried though about whether that might be a mistake. He had, he told me, a great capacity for self-deception. How could he be sure that his present wishes were not just another exercise in it? I told him I didn't think that was his biggest worry. In the first place, by his own admission, his life so far had been one vast tissue of mistakes: while it would no doubt be nice if he could avoid making one this time, it was obviously not a crucial consideration. He'd gotten this far in the thick of them; barring something a lot more unforeseen than his messing up personal relationships, he'd probably die at a ripe old age of something else entirely.

And as for the danger of self-deception, I told him not to worry about that either. If he was really as good at it as he said, he would never even figure out he was doing it. And if he wasn't, then sooner or later, he'd stop. Either way, he'd be ahead. But if he sat around just trying to take precautions instead of acting wholeheartedly on what he thought he wanted, he'd never get out of the cloud of irresolution in which he lived.

He professed a certain amount of dismay at that. Wasn't it irresponsible to sit so loose to precaution? Didn't we owe it to others to insure as much as possible against visiting mistakes on them?

I resisted the temptation to point out the self-deception involved in giving his habitual waffling the dignified name of caution. Instead, I conceded his point with one hand and took it back with the other. Of course we should try to avoid mistakes, but in the larger matters of life, it's not always easy to know in advance what the mistakes are. When the choice comes down to either acting at the risk of an error or not acting on the off chance of avoiding one, the first option at least has one knowable quantity: your action. The second has nothing you can set your mind to at all.

Take the Prodigal, I told him. His coming home from the far country—his re-exposing himself to all the problems with his father which, by a psychological inevitability, must have lain at the roots of his rebellion—could have been the biggest mistake of his life. And, in giving him an unqualified welcome, the father may have been letting himself in for nothing but *tsouris*. But the point of the story is that the possibility of anything's being a mistake was simply not allowed to influence the action. The accepter, in his freedom to be wrong, took in the accepted and gave him the same freedom. To wait for a world in which there are guarantees of being right is to wait too long for the world we have.

My friend was still not willing to put the subject down, though. He told me he once knew someone who said that we never make major mistakes except with people, or things, that really are not "our subject"; and that, as a corollary, you could always tell whether something really was your subject by the absence of major mistakes. Didn't that suggest that maybe marrying—or at least the people he had so far married—were just not his subject?

I had two reactions to that. The first was amazement at what people can say in front of others without the least awareness of what it must sound like to them. The woman who was, however loosely, his intended was actually holding his hand when he unlimbered that large-bore doubting piece. Since she didn't let it go, I took the liberty of observing that, even if he never did succeed in finding "his subject," he might just have been lucky enough this time to find someone who was actually willing to try to make him hers. Maybe it was the best he was going to do. After all, if the tone-deaf could get music into their homes by marrying singers, maybe the people-deaf could finally find a relationship in a similar way.

My second reaction, however, was consternation: the line he had just thrown me about making major mistakes only in things that aren't our subject was an old favorite of mine. Having never used it to defend inaction, though, I was surprised to have it turned against me. Some quick backing and filling was in order.

I told him I thought it was probably true, but that it was useful only after the fact of a mistake. It helped you to understand what went wrong and why—and it might even give you a few pointers about how to avoid the more damaging forms of inattention next time around. But as a way of discovering in advance what your subject was—or, worse yet, of deciding that x or y was not your subject—it didn't work.

In the first place, with a new subject, there were no mistakes before the fact on which to base the judgment. Furthermore, when the subject was another human being, it was by definition always new. The only basis on which you could decide beforehand that somebody wasn't your subject would be the fear of mistakes, and if you were going to put fear in first place, you would never do anything.

But even if you had failed before at something or someone, your mistakes were not the only factor in the situation. If other people were willing to overlook them or bear with them, things were obviously not desperate. And if you could manage to put up with them yourself, you could go right on claiming any subject you liked to be your own, even if everybody said it wasn't. After all, who made it a rule you couldn't fail? Certainly not anyone who ever tried to do anything. Maybe he was the Florence Foster Jenkins of matrimony: she couldn't sing any better than he could pick wives, but she never let it stop her.

As far as I could see, I told him, the most important thing in life was not waiting around till we found a subject so uniquely ours that it would elicit some mistake-free performance from us. It was to decide whom or what we thought we were after and then pay any price we had to, in money, mistakes or emotional wear and tear, to get it. That, I pointed out, was the biblical order. The world might wait for its heart to land before it puts its wherewithal down, but the scriptural rule was, where your treasure is, there shall your heart be also. Put up, and you'll be much less likely to shut up.

Suppose, though, he said, you just couldn't afford it? In his present state, financial and mental, he really didn't feel it would be right to spread himself as thin as another marriage would require.

At that point, my patience, if not my good humor, finally ran out. If that's the case, I said, he should rejoice because he had finally found his real subject. Its name was: Affording It. As far as I could see, that was the area in which he had never made a major mistake. Maybe he ought to stick with it. But just for the record, I added that being able to afford something wasn't the absolute he thought it was. He assumed that certain expenditures of himself were beyond his means because the nature of the universe made them so. I insisted that what was or wasn't beyond your means was just a matter of personal decision: if you set your minimum balance low enough, it was amazing what you could afford.

Could he for example, I asked him, afford to be dead? The answer was not only that he could (nobody bothers to tell a corpse he's overdrawn), but that he eventually would be whether he thought he could afford it or not. Since that much was certain, didn't it leave him free to decide the rest of his affordabilities for himself? If the final "mistake" of his life would absolve him of all insolvencies, however major, why did he have to go on fussing about the risk of minor ones? He could be as broke or as wrong or as mistaken as he chose to be. All he was doing by trying to bankroll himself was precluding the discovery of something that might possibly be worth being insolvent for. Why?

He said he didn't really know: the habit of fear, perhaps. Everybody had it. Didn't I?

I said, sure—possibly even worse than he did. But that wasn't the point. It wasn't a question of whether we felt the fear of mistakes but of whether we chose to trim our sails to it or not. The difference between him and me was not that I made fewer, but that I simply refused to let them be the ground of my self-acceptance. If God wouldn't let them matter, why should I?

He said that was all well and good, but what about other people? They sometimes made them matter with a vengeance. How did I manage to afford the nonacceptance they so freely handed out?

By deciding to, I told him; just as with everything else. I granted him, though, that it wasn't cheap. It could cost anybody a bundle of friends.

XII

REMARRIAGE & RESURRECTION

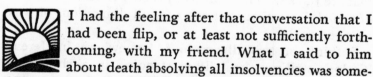I had the feeling after that conversation that I had been flip, or at least not sufficiently forthcoming, with my friend. What I said to him about death absolving all insolvencies was something I believed in deeply. For reasons of temperament, though, I skimmed over its ramifications. I have a constitutional aversion (based on either cowardice or compassion) to leading people suddenly into deep water. But whatever the case, I often end up leaving unsaid what I really have in mind. Just to avoid doing the same with you, therefore, let me spell out a few of the things I wished afterward I had said to him. Later, perhaps, you and I can pursue them in depth and at leisure; but to leave them simply unmentioned is a mistake that doesn't need repeating.

When I tossed in the example of his being able to "afford" to be dead, it was no mere throwaway illustra-

tion. As I see it, death is not an incident that ends relationships; rather, it is the constant condition of their
existence. It is the fundamental requirement, not only for
sustaining and restoring them, but even for bringing them
into being in the first place. Obviously, one of the senses
in which I'm using the word death is metaphorical: a
reference to the fact that the only way we can get rid of
the entail of guilt and error in our lives is to let go completely of the self that was responsible. There is no living
with the disasters of our history—at least no living that
isn't fakery. Nobody rises out of the unendurable and the
irremediable; he just sinks deeper under the weight. It's
only when he becomes as selfless as if he were dead that
resurrection to a new life becomes possible.

But if one of my meanings of death is metaphorical, the
other is perfectly literal: to me, the death that happens
once in a lifetime is in fact the pattern for the daily deaths
that are the key to life. Indeed, it's only from the starkness
of actual death that we learn the full dimensions of what
we need to do.

I think of two illustrations. Somewhere in Jeremy
Taylor's writings, he tells of standing in a churchyard
looking at the graves of two women he once knew—women
who had made each other's lives miserable with envy and
spite. But as he stood there, he had a feeling of calmness,
of absolution: the two lifetimes of mutual fear were over
at last. Death had finally declared peace in the war that
neither of them, while they lived, was willing to end. The
only sadness was that they had not voluntarily let it all go
sooner—that they had not died as effectively in their lives
as they did in their deaths.

The second illustration carries that even further. I
knew a man once—he was in his early forties, well married, well situated, surrounded by beautiful and talented

children—who was drinking himself down the drain. He responded to no known form of treatment, not psychiatry, not AA, not even the periodic shock treatments he received by way of wifely abandonment and weekends in jail. The nub of his problem, as he explained to me through more midnight visits and phone calls than I care to remember, was his father. The old man was . . . well, there were not many uncomplimentary things, from Autocrat to Well Poisoner, that he was not.

How true any of those charges was in strict justice, I never learned. All that mattered was that even if every one of them had been literally true, they could not have produced a more confused son, or a worse father-son relationship, than they did. There was, it seemed, no way out. Then, one day, his father died.

I suppose there's no way of making the rest of the story sound pretty, so I shall simply tell you what happened: from the day of the funeral forward, the son never drank again. His former problems, booze, bile and all, died in his father's death. When I came to ask myself why, the only answer I could think of was a heightening of Jeremy Taylor's graveyard meditation: death is indeed the great absolver; but it doesn't necessarily take two deaths to undo the failed history of a relationship. Even one will do; in fact, the partner in crime who dies first actually becomes the one who opens the way to reconciliation. That's not a flattering truth: we would no doubt much prefer it if our children, or our wives or our friends could get their lives together while we lived. But I think it is still a truth for all that: with alarming frequency, their problems with us end only when we do.

Unless, of course, we or they can manage some sufficiently extensive metaphorical deaths in the meantime. For if putting ourselves out of circulation is such a sover-

eign cure on a one-time basis, what might it not do as a
day-to-day tonic for our relationships? It's when you put
it that way that you begin to see some light.

Think, once again, of the Prodigal Son. If you look at
the parable closely, death is the very engine of the story.
The son admits his death to his sonship in the far country;
the father dies to all the righteous demands of fatherhood
and kisses his son without a single explanation, given or
received; even the fatted calf contributes a death to the
celebration. And when the elder brother (the only live,
and therefore wretched, character in the parable) com-
plains about the injustice of it all, his father insists that
death is the only consideration in the matter: "It was meet
that we should make merry and be glad; for this your
brother was dead and is alive again . . ." The father received his son out of nothing at his birth, and he receives
him back out of nothing in his death. Death and resurrection, he tells the boy's sour sibling, is the way these
things work.

Which may be why, when you think of it, people cry
at weddings—and why all genuinely new relationships
have such an air of going out of business about them. In
the Bible, for example, new beginnings are almost always
accompanied by the abolition of people's names—of their
former identities. Abraham stops being Abram. Jacob is
renamed Israel. Simon disappears into Peter, and Saul is
left behind on the Damascus road so that Paul can take
his place as the apostle of resurrection.

In other contexts, the death is symbolized differently,
but it's always there: the person baptized drowns to his
old life; the knight is ceremonially felled by his lord's
sword; the boy becomes a warrior in the tribe by an ordeal
that destroys his boyhood forever. But for most of us, marriage—even with its sentimental and sometimes sexist
overtones—remains the commonest sacrament of the death

that is the true ground of life: the man departs from father and mother and becomes one flesh with his wife; the father dies when he gives his daughter away.

Not surprisingly, it was Saint Paul who made the most of the sacramental connection. When he quoted the passage about leaving father and mother in the Epistle to the Ephesians, his mind leaped at once to the larger issue of death and resurrection. "This is a great mystery" (*mysterion*: the Greek theological word for sacrament). But then he added: "I'm actually talking about Christ and the church." Life, as he had come to experience it, was not a matter of Saul's getting his act together; it was one of letting it fall apart—of getting Saul out of the way so that Paul could rise. Even though marriage as such was not part of his own history, the death to old ties and old ways that it demanded—and above all, the rising to a new identity that it promised—struck him as a true sacrament of the way the universal order of relationships works.

It strikes me, though, that we can add something here. Apart from short-lived tears at weddings, we don't usually see marriage as a sacrament of death and resurrection. Our emphasis is far more on the strengthening of the grips we have on our being than it is on that letting go which is the only way the cosmos in fact produces new life.

In the case of beginning marriages, for example, we imagine that it's the deliberate cultivation of already known compatibilities that will be the key to marital success. With older, and perhaps tireder unions, we pin our hopes on the invention of techniques for openness and dialogue. For tottering ones, we have as many therapies as there are books on the subject. But in every case, we give the ultimately false impression that there will always be something that can be done. If this were a better world, no doubt there might be. But in the world as it is—where we regularly accumulate pasts that destroy our present—the only way our relationships survive is when someone finally recognizes there is nothing to do and lets that fact become fruitful in his death. Or, to tie the illustration to something I said earlier, it's not enough simply to get the future installed in the present of a marriage; the really crucial trick is to learn how to get the past out of it.

One of the commonplaces of old-fashioned theology was that death came into the world because of sin. In the newer theologies, that tended to be shelved, largely because people gave it an unimaginative, physical interpretation: they balked at the improbable prospect of Adam's dragging on through six thousand years of history.

But seen in a better light, it's nothing but a home truth: death is the only way sin can be undone. Evil abides. It slips irretrievably into an unchangeable past; but once it's there, it has all the rest of time to haunt the present. Impossible to abolish, impossible to forget, its power over us lasts as long as we ourselves do. Adam's real problem with a life that never ended would not have been its improbability; it would have been the certainty of six millennia of irremovable garbage. If death hadn't come along, he would have had to invent it. The only alternative would have been a world in which the damaged and damaging past reigned even more supreme than it does now.

Follow that out a bit as far as marriage is concerned. Since there are no couples anywhere without their fair share of such a past—or, to put it plainly, since there are no available candidates for marriage except sinners—do we not need most of all to reassert the centrality of death in dealing with such a situation? And if our view of the sacrament of marriage is too sentimental or too sanguine to reassert it for us, might it not possibly be that remarriage—with its inevitable and clear connection with death, literal or otherwise—is the most accessible sacrament of it we have?

No doubt that seems odd. The long history of antipathy between the Holy Estate and its reputedly less than holy counterpart does not at first blush give much hope that they might be manifestations of the same thing. But to my mind, and I think to the minds of most who remarry, that is exactly the case. For no matter how it occurs, whether after widowhood or after divorce, remarriage plainly involves a past that will not yield to efforts to set it right. That's true in all relationships, of course; but only in remarriage is it so clearly proclaimed as a beginning instead of an end. A second marriage, at least before it settles back into being just another marriage, is nothing less than a resurrection out of death. If that mystery is indeed the key to reclaiming the past, we couldn't be hunting for it in a better place.

Perhaps, though, if we think just a bit more about the unique kind of death involved in a divorce, we can get on still better with the hunt. As a start, therefore, consider the word itself. Its common meaning is imprecise: divorce, as we ordinarily use it, refers to a single act by which a presumably live relationship between two people is terminated. That usage, however, has unrealistic consequences. It leads not only moralists, but all of us, to assume that if, in any given case, the act of legal divorcing could somehow have been avoided, the marriage involved would still be alive. If John and Mary had gone to counseling instead of court, they wouldn't have caused the mayhem they did.

But if we knew them well enough—perhaps even better than they knew themselves—we know that's almost never true. In reality, they were apart long before they parted. And interestingly enough, the word divorce is quite patient of that understanding. By its etymology, it refers simply to separation—to a going off in disparate directions that can happen whether two people formalize it before a judge or not. When the word is used in that way, a "divorce action" becomes, not the cause of a divorced relationship, but simply the recognition that one already exists. It is, in other words, not the moment of their marriage's expiration, but the day of its burial. The decision involved was to end a wake, not a life.

That, incidentally, points up why it is usually so hard for legally divorced people to enter with any deliberate speed into a relationship of "continuing concern" for each other. Their goal, for as long as they made any effort to stay together, was to hold onto whatever shreds of life they thought they could find. However, when they finally bring themselves to the point of recognizing the death of their relationship, a new goal has to be found. And the only realistic one for either of them at that juncture is to move on to recognizing that not only the relationship but he himself has died.

But for as long as one or both continue to clutch at vestiges of the old life (whether in nostalgia or in anger), there can be no new basis for continuing concern. The only thing the clutching does is condemn them to a continual pursuit of the goal of "living"—and under the very conditions that made it impossible to achieve: if they could have concerned themselves for each other in their marriage, they would have. But obviously, they didn't; and equally obviously, until their personal deaths are accepted, they never will. If people haven't made a life out of their lives, they simply have no material other than their deaths to offer up for the job.

If all that strikes you as too abstruse to be called obvious, think again. One of the commonest experiences of anyone who deals with the divorced is to find that they recognize, albeit miserably and incongruently, that death must somehow be dealt with. Either they decide that the offending spouse has to be executed, mentally if not physically ("I would just love to blow his brains out"); or, despairing of such pointless and dangerous enterprises, they think of doing themselves in. Suicide is practically the small talk of the divorced.

Unfortunately, those who counsel them are often no help. Even if friends and relatives manage to avoid the mistake of cheering for aimless acts of mental murder, they almost always fall into the trap of simply and uncritically discouraging the person who proposes suicide. The lament, "If only I were dead, he wouldn't bother me," elicits from them not a helpful, discerning response, but two Valiums, a glass of water and the uncomprehending advice not to talk like that.

Talking like that, however, is just what is called for. I spoke with a woman once who came here in a crumpled heap at the bottom of a divorce. She was still trying, after a year without her husband, to hold onto the life she once had. Every meeting, every conversation with him, confronted her with the death of her marriage; but because she had not accepted that death for herself, each encounter threw her into deeper panic. Finally—and, of course, guiltily—she began to think of suicide.

Her friends, predictably, had shied away in alarm; so I decided to take a different approach. She was, I suggested, on exactly the right track. In fact, she had her hand on the very truth she most needed. The only thing she had to do was learn to pick it up by the proper handle. I said she was correct to feel that the only workable course of action was to make herself dead to a relationship that was dead already; but I added that it was by no means necessary to get herself that way by such an undiscriminating device as suicide.

I asked her whether there was anything in her present life she enjoyed being alive for. At first—caught as she was in the lush swamp of despair—she said there was nothing at all. A little conversation, however, brought her out of that: she enjoyed her children, her work—even, it finally came out, the new man in her life.

There was the opening I had been looking for. If that was so, I urged, why didn't she consider the possibility of a more selective suicide? Why kill off all those good parts of her life when she could, if she made up her mind to, die only to the wretched ones? The next time she was tempted to give artificial respiration to the corpse of her marriage—to meet her husband for a hopeful drink, or to involve herself in his financial confusions—why didn't she first picture to herself her own tombstone and then respond only as she would if she were under it? She was surprised. Did I mean, not respond at all? Well, I said, how else would she respond if she had actually stuck her head in the oven? Admittedly, it might take some discipline for a while—and she might be tempted to revive prematurely at times; but it was definitely preferable to the overkill she had in mind.

I pointed out that if her relationship with her husband had been manageable on the basis of her being alive to it, she would long ago have managed it that way. Now, however, there were no old patterns left that would work. When and if some new ones appeared, they would come, not out of her doomed efforts to hold onto a vanished fullness, but simply out of her offering of an emptiness sufficient to permit a genuine resurrection. Far from being off the mark in talking about wanting to die, she had been right on. All I was urging on her, I said at the end, was to try it where it might do her, and everybody else, some good.

Surprisingly—to herself at least—she left the house feeling much lighter than when she came. The thought of having her own selectively located tombstone was a load off, rather than on, her chest. I recognize, though, that you may find the subject a bit weighty for the middle of the day, so I shall put it down. With only the proviso that I may heft it again later, on we go to other things.

XIII

REMARRIAGE & FRIENDS

Let me give the oven another ten seconds' worth of heat and then let's get out of the kitchen for awhile. If I'm not mistaken, the barometer is starting to drop. We've had, I think, not only the best part of the day as far as weather is concerned, but also all the Indian summer we're likely to have this year. Time to crank up the wood stove in the living room. After that, you can sit and talk to Madeleine while I take my shower.

What's that? Will she actually appear? Oh, yes. Building a fire is the infallible device for securing her presence. She may not stay put for long, of course: her mutable moon, she claims, makes her prone to frequent disappearances. But enjoy her while you can. I'll be back shortly.

* * *

Yes, I know. I passed her on her way out to the post office. I suggest, however, that you do not expect her to be back in anything even vaguely resembling shortly. My standard computation for determining her ETA is to figure out how long it would take a normal human being to do her stated errand, plus a couple of unstated ones and a visit to a friend—and then to add two hours to the result. We'll be lucky if we see her by mid-afternoon. I guarantee, however, that she'll be back by the time the loaves come out of the oven. Moon in Sagittarius or not, she always manages to get a fix on hot bread and butter.

But what, if I may ask, did you two talk about while I was gone? She seemed slightly . . . well, steamed, on the way out.

Oh. You picked up where my remarks left off and asked her whether we really had all that much trouble with rejection by old friends. And she told you: Plenty. Say no more. I know the conversation well.

Would I say that she exaggerated the problem? No. It has taken my tightrope-walking mind awhile to realize it, but Madeleine never exaggerates. She simply says whatever she thinks without bothering to keep her balance. If she approves of something, she dives wholeheartedly into praise; if not, she plunges with equal verve into condemnation. And in any given instance, she's quite likely to do both in quick succession. I once suggested that if she'd be a little more restrained, she might not have to go flying all over the tent like that. "Look at me," I said; "most of the time, I'm right up there, rock steady on the old high wire." "Terrific," she said; "think of all the other parts of the circus you miss."

Circus or not, though, rejection by old friends is one of the biggest crosses in any remarriage, and it occurs to me it might make a good topic on which to round the bend from the problems of the past to the problems of the present. We've looked backward at divorce long enough. It's time to talk about how you live with the results.

For openers, therefore, some rules for survival under Old Friendly Fire.

(These, by the way, are my rules, not Madeleine's. My first instinct is always to duck; hers, to toss grenades back where they came from. The truth, no doubt, lies somewhere between us, but since she's gone out, you'll have to triangulate it by yourself.)

Rule 1. Since I am free to make all kinds of mistakes and still think myself acceptable, so are my friends. If they have committed the error of choosing sides between me and my first wife—or worse yet, of not choosing my side —they have their reasons and it's not going to do me any good to say they should have done otherwise. I can control only my attitude, not theirs; if I think acceptance is so all-fired important, the least I can do is keep rejection out of my own backyard.

Corollary. There are no ex-friends, any more than there are ex-wives or ex-husbands. The prefix is a pretense, and a transparent one at that. Even the phrase "former friends" reeks of self-pity and righteous indignation; exing them simply adds blackwashing history to the list of crimes. Call them unfriendly friends, rotten friends, or even enemies, if you like; at least that posits a bad relationship rather than a nonexistent one. But don't make believe they're not still part of your life. They bother you; therefore, they are.

Rule 2. Don't let the few—or even the many—old friends who reject you trick you into tucking your tail between your legs with those who don't. Some does not mean all; but if you go around complaining you're a poor soul who hasn't a real friend in the world, that could very well end up being the truth.

Corollary. While you're at it, don't ask your remaining good friends to do what you're complaining about in your bad ones: choose sides, build walls, end relationships. They've accepted you precisely because they've refused to do any bookkeeping on your case. Don't urge them to begin. It's one thing for friends to love you despite your difficulties, but it's quite another to ask them to do it because of them. Enjoy them, but don't try to enlist them.

Rule 3. Don't shut anyone out yourself. First of all, it's waste motion: if your old friends have closed the door on you, your slamming it on them isn't going to separate you any more than you already are. All you do by that is double the number of people it's going to take to get that door open. But second, it's often just a peevish gesture at finalizing something that might not be final at all. People sometimes lose their reasons for finding others unacceptable: Mary Backstage (noble wife) cuts off her divorced friends; if she ever becomes an ignoble divorcée, though, guess who she phones. How nice, if she can find one who doesn't hang up.

Rule 4. In the meantime, make new friends. But remember that the newness has to come as much from you as from them. Very often, they will be your first clear shot at a relationship from which bookkeeping can be completely absent. Don't mess it up by slipping back into audits—either of them or of yourself. Good friendships are beyond reasons, so don't expect any. And above all, don't ever think you can give them.

Rule 5. Ah, but that is far too casual a beginning for the supreme rule of all—the rule which, if kept, produces tranquillity, order, good digestion and pleasant dreams, but which, if broken, lets loose all the powers of hell.

Let me give it therefore a more imposing exordium:

Regula V
Rule of Rules, Principle of Principles,
Canon of Canons, Law of Laws.

Don't listen to a damned thing anybody tells you about anyone.

This, obviously, is the Commandment against Gossip, formulated from the point of view of the subject, target or victim of the crime. It needs no subdividing and it has no corollaries. On its face, in fact, it is so simple and obvious a truth that the most remarkable thing about it is that it needs to be formulated at all. As advice, it's on a par with telling people not to touch hot stoves: one warning early in life, plus a single miserable experience, should be all anyone needs to have done with it for good.

In practice, however, most of us never stop being blistered by it, so a little analysis of the problem may be helpful. If you continually came to me complaining of burned hands, I could only conclude that something in your thinking needed correcting. Either your knowledge of just what a working stove could do was deficient, or your view of your own capacity for taking the heat was overblown. Or both. In any case, comment can't hurt.

Let's talk about the nature of the stove first. In the usual view, gossip is seen as a shortcut for communicating information. Your friend Sarah tells your friend Martha what she thinks of you. Martha, in turn, informs you—and you, assuming you have heard what Sarah thinks, proceed into the slough of despond, the vale of tears or the desert of anger, depending. You might, of course, hesitate a bit. There is always the possibility that Martha's information is incorrect. But that's hardly any comfort: all it does is make you dubious of her goodwill instead of Sarah's—or of her general intelligence, which is almost as bad. However you decide the question of the truth or falsity of the gossip, therefore, there is no way of feeling good about it.

Your mistake, of course, was in accepting the usual view of gossip as information, and then applying to it the test of truth or falsehood you would normally apply to any other assertion: namely, if it's false you can write it off, but if it's true you have to take it seriously. Nor are you alone in that error. Ninety-nine people out of a hundred, if they are told they're passing on gossip, will answer, "It's not gossip; it's true. I heard it with my own ears."

That, however, is to overlook completely the real nature of gossip. It's as if someone were to claim that a black stove will burn you but a white one will not. If you've got a roaring fire going, the color of the outside is irrelevant to its capacity for damage. Likewise, if you've got a friendship-destroying communications system going, it makes little difference whether the messages that run along it are true or false. The system can do its nasty work with either.

And a friendship destroyer is precisely what it is. Genuine information (good or bad, true or false) always has a distinguishing feature: it is passed between two people who inhabit the same world. What they have most deeply in common is not their words but their presence to each other—a presence which makes even a lie a form of personal encounter. But gossip, by definition, is a communication between people in different worlds. What Sarah said about you was said in a world from which you were absent. She was, literally enough, behind your back. And what Martha told you about her was likewise out of context. You might argue, of course, that a really good friend would always have you in her world even if you weren't there. And you'd be right. The greatest friends don't gossip. But great friends are rare, and nobody should be too surprised at being left out of a world now and then.

The important thing (besides obeying Rule five and not listening to a damned bit of it) is to convince yourself of the fact that your trouble is coming from separated worlds, and then to try to put them back together. Take what Sarah said, for example. Had you been there at the time, there are three entirely possible outcomes that might have taken the place of the impossibility you're now dealing with. Either she would not have said it at all in your presence, or she would have said it differently, or she would have said it as quoted to you. But whichever it was, you would not have the problem you have now. For even if she said the very same dreadful thing, the fact of her saying it to your face—in the same world—would have led to confrontation, not separation. You could have blasted her and, for all you know, come out better friends than ever.

The most important thing to know about gossip, therefore, is that it's unreal. And it makes everybody who indulges in it unreal too. I have known some champion gossips in my day and the one thing that stands out about them is that they have no world of their own to share with anybody. They have lived so long transmitting messages from separated worlds that they themselves have become little more than spaces full of echoes. Talking to one of them is like biting into a chocolate-covered liquid cherry that someone drained the center out of: once you get past the outside, there's nothing there.

What's all that got to do with remarriage? Everything, because for all practical purposes, there's no way remarried people can avoid being the subjects of gossip. If their friends don't bring them tales of who said what about them, their children, their parents, their siblings or their neighbors will. The only cure for it is an ironbound refusal to deal with any secondhand information at all—and a willingness to pay the price of looking stupid for refusing.

The world, in its mindless way, will chide you for minimizing the "danger" it thinks you're in: "I hate to tell you this, but Harry said if you marry Fred, he'll sue for custody of the children. I thought you ought to be forewarned." But look at it this way: what's wrong with minimizing the danger? What do they want you to do, maximize it? If Harry's really going to give you a hard time, you'll soon enough have to deal with him yourself. But if he's not—if the threat was just the product of four full scotches and one empty world—why shouldn't you simply ignore it?

Therefore, *Rules 6 to six million: If it hasn't been said to you in person, it hasn't been said at all.*

And for the master *Corollary* to the lot of them: Your number's in the phone book. For seven firsthand digits, anybody can find your world. Even heavy breathing is preferable to all that secondhand gas.

XIV

REMARRIAGE & CHILDREN

There's a category of friends, however, that I haven't said nearly enough about: children. I lumped them with parents, siblings and neighbors a few minutes ago, but they stand in a unique relationship to a remarriage. While others have the option of being simply in your world or out of it, the assembled or scattered offspring of twice-married parents are trapped into being halfway in and halfway out of two worlds at the same time. That's partly due to the developing nature of the beasts: even the once-married have to put up with their children's friable and unpredictable loyalties. When you remarry, though, you have the problem in spades: your children, like everyone's, are not ready decisively to become either your friends or your enemies; but because they hear from both camps, the decision is prematurely urged upon them. Divorce may have relieved you of the burden of dealing with your former spouse's world, but only rarely—and then, usually, sadly—does it relieve the children.

But contrary to what you might expect, I'm not going to talk about the effect of remarriage on children. For one thing, the subject has been done to death—or at least to the point of scaring the living daylights out of anyone who reads the statistics. For another, it is such a vexed and varied subject that I can think of almost nothing specific that would apply from one situation to the next. Children in remarriages come at such different ages and in such diverse recombinations of number, gender and case that there is only the smallest likelihood that what I happen to know firsthand would look to you like help at all.

Therefore, I will say only this about what remarrying may do to them: you'll never know till it's been done, so don't let the fear of causing problems give you second thoughts when you should be having first ones. Childhood, if you will cast your mind back, is a sea of problems anyway. Concern over whether your remarriage is responsible for creating them makes about as much sense as worrying whether your emptying a coke bottle into the ocean contributes to the flooding in a hurricane. Obviously, it does. But if you think that taking six ounces of remarriage out of their lives is going to make their low-lying basements any less flood-prone, you owe yourself another think.

The idea of getting un-remarried to solve juvenile problems probably takes some kind of prize for ineffectuality in the Things Done for the Sake of the Children contest. It's second only, perhaps, to the notion of staying married on their behalf. The fact is that by the time they are four or five we have done them so much irremediable harm and good that our subsequent decisions, right or wrong, about their welfare have hardly a chance of catching up. If we care for them, we just love them as we can and hope to heaven the treatment isn't worse than the disease.

Which, of course, it often is. Human beings, allowed within reaching distance, give each other problems faster than cats shed hair. If there's anything to be said on the subject of remarriage's effect on children, it should probably be a warning against canvassing the question at all. What's needed is not, "Has Daddy hurt Beth?" or "Is Stepmommy good for Georgie?" There are as many answers to those as there are respondents with axes to grind, and your chances of getting one that proclaims you innocent of causing problems are next to nil. Besides, innocence is for kids; remarriage is growing-up time for everybody.

Therefore, what you ought to say is, "Look, kiddies, we're all in this together. I'm a problem; you're a problem. It would be nice if we weren't, but in the world we have it's a bit late in the day for that. So let's just skip the subject of how bad or sad or mad it is that we have to deal with each other. Even if we're all wrong, we've got to operate on the assumption that it's all right for us to have problems. There are, in fact, only two no-no's here: telling somebody he shouldn't have the problems he has; and thinking you can't complain about yours. We can reason, argue, scream or punch. If that doesn't look much like the peaceable kingdom, it's the only road that's open to it at the moment. Someday all the parental wolves are going to lie down comfortably with all their disgruntled kids. But until we make it there, we're not going to fake it here. Come out of your corner swinging if you must; but for all our sakes, come on out."

Having said that, though, it seems to me that the biggest fact about our offspring is that they're going to outlast us. Like seeds, they have a durability—at least for now—that the old plants who produced them will never match again. Accordingly, the rest of my remarks will not be about what remarriage might do to children but about some of the mischief children all too easily make in remarriage. It may not be the usual way to pick the subject up, but it's mine. At this stage, one more left-handed pitch can't hurt.

XV

CHILDREN & REMARRIAGE

The first thing about it is that children are, by nature, aliens to a remarriage. In many ways, of course, all human beings are aliens to each other; but when people remarry, they make a conscious attempt to break out of the alienation that dogged their past. Even more so than in a youthful first marriage, they try to set their old, separate ways aside and make a new, more intimate life together. Eve Smith and Adam Jones propose a new Eden in which the Smithness and Jonesness they mismanaged the first time around will be kept outside the garden wall.

But however successfully they themselves transcend the Smith-Jones syndrome, it's still there; and when the children of their previous unions arrive on the scene, it's aggravated mightily. That's obvious even when only one of them brings children to the remarriage, but it's especially clear when each brings a set: to Eve, Adam's children appear to be in the tertiary phase of galloping Jonesness; to Adam, hers have terminal cases of the Smiths. Unless they're both forewarned and forearmed, the likelihood of wedges being driven between them is so high it's almost a certainty.

For one thing, the younger generations of the clans have no compelling interest in papering over differences. Like all human beings, each group is convinced that only its way of doing things is truly human. To the Smiths, the Joneses come from some deeply retarded planet where nothing is done right: they eat no normal food, read no interesting books, make no sensible remarks and, crime of crimes, at Christmas they put flashing lights on the tree. When Eve suggests to them that they ought to try at least to be pleasant to their step-siblings, they can only conclude she has renounced her membership in the race. And if, God forbid, Adam suggests it, it just proves he never belonged anyway.

Unfortunately, it's seldom left at that. The one compelling interest they have—always, at first, and often enough, for a good while afterward—is staying tight with the parent they know. Hence their penchant for wedge driving. Some children, of course, do it consciously, even diabolically: they'll use anything that comes to hand to pry Eve from Adam's side to theirs. But malice aforethought is by no means necessary. The wedge between any two people is always there, just under the wallpaper job. A tap now and then is all it takes to drive it deeper. The couple may try as hard as they like to leave it alone themselves, but they should never be surprised at the rips that even innocent knocking about can produce.

That happens, of course, with all children, even when they're the joint offspring of a remarriage—even, in fact, when they're the issue of a marriage that never breaks up. There isn't a child in the world who doesn't identify more

with one parent than another. Therefore, self-interest being the major concern it is, there isn't one who won't,
from time to time, give his favorite a shove in the direction of what he considers sanity. But if the Smith-Jones
syndrome is to be kept from developing into a standoff
between the couple themselves, there are some don'ts
about their children they need to keep in mind.

First, don't expect children to have your reasons for
accepting your spouse. Human beings have a congenital
difficulty understanding what people see in each other,
and they have an equally deep reluctance to take anybody
else's word for it. If children ever do endorse your vision,
it will be for their reasons, not yours. In the meantime,
the best any remarried couple can do is skip the selling
job and concentrate on keeping their own reasons intact.

That being the case, don't be suckered into losing your
vision by letting your children—or anybody else—turn it
into a test of your loyalty to them. Loyalty is a large subject and, paradoxically, the two most important comments
that need to be made about it are almost diametrically
opposed. The first is that if you're not willing to say where
your primary loyalty lies, you're almost certain to end up
with no loyalties at all. Scripture says surprisingly little
that's positive about marriage, but one of the things it
says loud and clear is that two people can cleave to each
other only by cleaving to nobody else. "Forsaking all
others" is a phrase whose meaning has practically been
obscured by merely sexual interpretations; but by definition, it applies straight across the board: in the case of
first marriages, to fathers and mothers, brothers and aunts;
and in the case of remarriages, to friends, wives, husbands
and children as well.

The saddest thing about so many remarried people is
that, having paid the high price of all those forsakings—
in many cases, twice—they are tricked into welshing on

their new first loyalty because they're afraid of losing their children's allegiance. It's sad because they end up paying an even higher price: at the cost of the only allegiance they ever had a chance of managing, they try to buy one over which they have no control. Children's loyalties are ultimately not parents' business. Take care of your own as best you can, then, and sit loose to the rest. You bought what you bought; be happy with that.

But if it sounds hardhearted to insist so heavily on the first loyalty of the remarried to each other—if you think it would be a better world if the subject never came up—I will agree with you. My paradoxical second comment about it is that you should try your best to keep anyone —especially children—from testing you on it at all. People question your loyalty chiefly when their noses are out of joint; that is, when they have already decided you've flunked the test. It doesn't matter that it's the easiest thing in the world for the children of a remarriage to put themselves into that position, wittingly or not. The point is that it's a loser's game; the only good move is to call it off. It takes nerve—specifically, it takes a willingness to pay the price of rejection—but once they ask you to choose between your spouse and them, there's only one way to handle it. You say, as kindly but as clearly as possible, "Look, love, this is a question I don't want to hear and you don't need to ask. If you insist on my ranking my loyalties, you're going to get a list you won't like. So back off. You're on the list, and you're the only you that's there. But if you're not happy about where you are, that's your business, not mine. Why don't we both quit while we're ahead and have a beer?"

That, I suppose, applies mostly to teenage children and older, but there's another don't that applies to all of them: if they're not supposed to run loyalty tests on you, don't you run any on them. Specifically, don't try to get them to choose sides between you and your former spouse. Obviously, that's bad for them—and the younger they are, the worse it probably is. But it's just as dangerous for you because it inevitably involves you in the unreal world of gossip.

So often—whether or not there has been contention over child support, custody or visitation rights—former spouses encourage children to run messages between them, or even to act as spies. But however great the temptation may be to get all that fascinating information, remember that, for you, it's no more genuine than any other second-hand communication. What Adam Jones's first wife says to his son was not said to Adam. If he pumps it out of the boy, he deserves all the rusty water he gets. Because even though the child lives in two worlds, his father and mother have only one apiece. If they want to put them together, let them talk to each other, not through an intermediary. Above all, let them not try to control the child's attitudes or behavior when he's in the world of the former spouse.

As I said, the danger to the child in all that meddling and talebearing is more obvious than the peril it poses for the two separated parents. If I had to give it a name, I would call it a foreign-affairs blunder—a political miscalculation by which two supposedly sovereign states turn over to an inexperienced and possibly adventurous third party the right to enunciate or even to define their intentions. There is hardly a child in the world, of any age, who is too dense to appreciate the power that accrues to him when he is made a go-between. He becomes the authority on mommy to daddy; he bears the official word to daddy on what mommy is up to. It's heady stuff, and there are few children who can't be hooked by it.

If you perpetuate the blunder, before you know it, you

will have a spurious-information junkie on your hands—
a pusher, in fact, who, to support his power habit, will sell
you anything that seems to turn you on. And since bad
news always has more of a kick than good, you will find
more and more of it being delivered, until in the end you
yourself are hooked on the downers.

There's only one cure. You have to tell your source
you're not in the market any more; and then you have to
master the temptation for an information fix every time
it arises. Or, to change the metaphor, you have to take as
your watchword the reply of the prizefighter to the trainer
who told him, as he slumped in his corner between
rounds, that his opponent had never laid a glove on him:
"Well, then, keep an eye on the referee," he said; "somebody in there is beating the hell out of me."

But let's move on. The next don't is about children and
money: don't be aced into a hole over financial arrange-
ments about child support or educational expenses. If they
can be made—and if they can be kept, by you or by your
former spouse—just be happy that somebody gets to play
the role of good guy. But if they can't be, or aren't, don't
spend even a minute making anybody (yourself included)
a bad guy. You separated to become sovereign states. The
posture of disgruntled dependence that defaulted-on financial assistance puts you in is not conducive to enjoying
your liberty.

In the first place, it tricks you back into cost counting.
At the high emotional and monetary price of a divorce,
you bought your freedom to lead a new life. But now, under the cover of "protecting the children's interests," you
begin counting pennies again. Having acted on the principle that nothing was too dear to keep you from your
remarriage (and paid your new partner the ultimate compliment in the process), you drift into saying that you
have discovered a loss that makes you unhappy in the

midst of all your gains. And that's not a compliment; it's just an indirect way of telling somebody he's not enough for you.

A little judicious fuss, of course, does no harm. Raise the subject once or twice if you like. But if it gets you nowhere, drop it. Because, in the second place, it doesn't matter as much as you think it does and it's seldom worth the trouble it gives you. Child support, whatever it is, has a way of being both too much and too little all at once: too much for the way they (mostly don't) eat, and too little for the way they wear out their clothes and their keepers. And college—that quasi-metaphysical necessity for which even the once-married mortgage their lives—is hardly the unmixed blessing we con ourselves into thinking it is.

Quite apart from the fact that a higher education often turns out to be nothing more than four years of thirteenth grade—and to qualify its products chiefly for unemployment—there is nothing wrong with telling a child he's going to have to get his on his own. Just do it without spreading guilt on anybody—not on your former spouse, not on yourself, not on the child. We keep our children adolescents far too long as it is. What they need most is to take over the credits and debts of their own performances as soon as possible. Handing them someone else to blame for their not going to college is no help. Admittedly, it may keep them on your side. But it may also keep them *at* your side longer than you can stand. Look ahead then: if you don't want a thirty-five-year-old kid around your neck, don't encourage an eighteen-year-old not to be an adult.

Lists of don'ts, however, become depressing if they get much longer than this, so let me end with just one more: no matter whose children are with you in your remarriage, don't try to enforce the desiderata of a new nuclear family upon them. A few simple rules of sane community living, perhaps; but even there, don't expect much more than a fairly relaxed commune to come of it. For one thing, the nuclear family is by no means as unqualifiedly desirable as its enthusiasts pretend. Very often, it's just another people-stifling angel who demands worship when individuals should be getting the attention. But for another, it's a demand you have no power to back up.

Once again, it's you who have the most to lose. Their game may be threatened a bit by the one big happy family pitch, but you can all too easily have your whole season ruined by it. Because no matter how earnestly you hymn the virtues of familial togetherness, the fact remains that the collection of people you've got on your hands are not one family, they're two. Worse yet, if you push too hard even for the lower good of community, the children involved can simply refuse to give it houseroom. The lesson to be learned, I suppose, is the slightly cynical but ultimately saving rule of Saint-Exupéry's *Little Prince*: never give an order unless you're sure it will be obeyed. Authority has about as much chance against noncompliance as ice cream has under a hot water tap. If you want to hold onto it, you've got to keep things cool.

The last word on the subject, therefore, is not a don't but a do: offer all your children, step or otherwise, friendship—and let it go at that. Adam Jones's Smithchildren already have a daddy; whatever paternal hash needs settling is on that gentleman's stove, not Adam's. And likewise with Eve. "Parenting" may be a dreadful neologism, but the job it denominates is the all-time dreadfulness winner anyway. Why anyone who has taken an honest look at his first performance at it—let alone anyone who was excused from it—would even think of being a parent when he could be a friend is simply a mystery. Arranging deck chairs on the *Titanic* is one thing; but putting in an application for the job after the iceberg has hit—and while there's a helicopter waiting to take you off . . .

Remarriage may or may not be the triumph of hope over experience, but re-parenting is pure disaster. Maybe, with our own children, we never will escape the curse of the job; even there, though, the sooner we try to be friends to them, the better off we'll all be. But with stepchildren we have a chance to do it sooner still.

Madeleine has a son and I have a daughter, both of whom live with us. I hated the way he stripped the finish off my omelet pan when he scrambled eggs; she hated the way her stepdaughter left the living room . . . but let me confine the illustration to my own case. Since Madeleine was even more tired than I was of being a parent (exhaustion is sometimes the mother of growth), she refused my request that she speak to her son like a Dutch mommy and tell him to keep his hands off my prize pan. "Speak to him yourself," she said. "But since you can't possibly lecture him like a daddy and be believed, why don't you just figure out what you'd say to a friend who'd done the same job on your pan and say *that* to him?"

And so I figured: a friend would have gotten a cheerfully informative description of how too much moving about of the eggs destroys the fragile coating of oil; next would have come a slightly exaggerated account of the labor involved in restoring the finish, followed by a winsome practicum on the actual cooking of scrambled eggs and a gentle request to keep all of the above in mind the next time he used, as he was of course most welcome to, my favorite omelet pan.

And so I said that. And contrary to all the expectations I had from twenty-five years of exploding at children, my stepson has taken excellent care of the pan ever since—even to the point of lecturing his sister about it as if he were her father. Ah, well. We learn, it seems, only one generation at a time; but at least sometimes we learn. I commend the procedure to you. If being a friend works even on a felony like that, think what it might do with such misdemeanors as dropping out, marrying wrong or ruining their careers.

XVI

REMARRIAGE & RELIGION

 Come back out to the kitchen with me for a few minutes. The bread has to be shaped into loaves along about now if it's going to be done in high time for Madeleine's due season.

What shape loaves? Small, freestanding ones, completely covered with sesame seeds: submarines, if you like. Do I use those special baking sheets that look like sections of half-round gutter? No. If you make your bread with high gluten flour and knead it long enough, they're quite unnecessary. People are always amazed at the loaves I get—except certain naturalness buffs, who claim they look too commercial. I just smile and correct them: "Not commercial. Professional."

How do I get the sesame seeds to stick? Ah, I can see you are a true student. But I must warn you. I am a compulsive teacher: don't ask me questions unless you're prepared for an avalanche of answers. In this case, though, you're safe enough. I beat an egg white with a little water; then, as soon as I've shaped the loaves, I bathe them in the egg wash, let them drain a bit on the counter and then roll them in a pan of sesame seeds till they're coated. After that, I give them plenty of rising time and, just before baking, I make one long, shallow cut down the center of each with a straight razor. Simple, no? What else would you like to know?

Could you use an ordinary knife? Sure, but it would have to be a lot sharper than most people's, if it weren't simply to mangle the loaves. Better to use a single-edge blade. I just happen to like the razor: it was my great-grandfather's. I know it's sharp because I use it every day. Unless it gets lost, I'll probably be able to pass it on to my great-grandchildren. It's certainly not going to wear out. I've had a full beard for years: all I shave is the bottom quarter inch of my upper lip. What else can I tell you about?

Well! How long have you been nursing *that* question? You would like to know, since I am still a priest in good standing and apparently a practicing Christian, what I have to say about all the harsh things the Bible says about divorce and remarriage. Ah! That gets us back on the track with a vengeance, doesn't it? But since you insist . . .

Breadmaking may be my hobby and remarriage my way of life; but theology is my *subject*. On this one, you really do get an avalanche.

Just to take the curse off it, though, let me cast my answer in the form of a long, slow curve.

You refer to "what the Bible says about divorce and remarriage." Stop right there. Scripture says many things about many subjects, and on some of them it has the disconcerting habit of contradicting itself right and left. The

Old Testament, for example, allows divorce—at least for men. The New Testament, admittedly, takes a dimmer view of it, and so it's to that I assume you're referring: Jesus' words to the effect that the remarriage of divorced persons constitutes adultery.

Now. One way of going about responding to such a hard line is to point out that it occurs only a couple of times—and even then, only in answer to some fairly tricky and hostile questions. Some people even go so far as to suggest that the tone, if not the substance of the reply, is probably a gloss reflecting the ethics of the early church rather than something he actually said.

I, however, have never liked that approach. Having long ago accepted the idea that Scripture is the Word of God, I am reluctant to interpret it by culling the bits that give me trouble into a bin marked: Not the Word of God. Since the Bible is the only record we have of what Jesus said, I can't see much solid ground for picking and choosing between the things it says he said. Nevertheless, that by no means makes me a fundamentalist. Even if I can't rule out any of the parts, I still feel quite free to pick and choose when it comes to the way I myself am going to think about the whole.

Accordingly, my first stab at the subject goes like this: Jesus, and everything he says, is the Word of God to us. Specifically, therefore, his discomfiting remarks about remarriage being tantamount to adultery are nothing less than the Father's Word on the subject. Having said that, however, it leaves you with at least two other topics open for discussion: what a Word is; and, in particular, whether the fact of its being a Father's Word has any bearing on the case.

As to the first, a word—at least in the sense that Scripture is a word—is not just an isolated vocable; it's a communication. The word "step," for example, has no particular meaning to me until I hear it in a larger word: "Step up and collect your winnings," "There's a step missing from your argument," "Watch your step!" But by the same token, a communication is not just an isolated sentence. It's part of a larger and longer dialogue between two parties. And when that dialogue becomes large and long enough, it will always be true not only that the same word will be used with different meanings, but, much more to the point, that different, even opposed communications will be used to keep the rich, but ultimately single meaning of the whole dialogue from getting lost.

If that sounds complicated, it isn't. You tell your child, "Lying is all wrong." But since he's already lied and said he's sorry, what do you say to him? You tell him, "It's all right."

Simple, no? Only a literalist could have problems with that. Obviously, you said two opposed things; but equally obviously, you said them for the same reason: you cared for him. It just so happened that because he didn't care enough for himself, you had to hit him with two words at once on the subject: the first, that he should have cared more than he did; and the second, that you're not going to stop caring just because he does. In your mind, in other words, there is no real contradiction in what you said. However, if you turn the matter around and look at it from the child's point of view, you'll see something that really is complicated—and that sheds light on our problems with Scripture. For to the receiver of those apparently forked-tongued communications, it always seems as if there is no way they can both be true—as if he had to decide, on some basis external to himself, which one of them is false. If the father really means the word about good behavior, then the one about indulgence can't be true; if the forgiving word is serious, the other can't matter at all.

But since that can't possibly be the case—each word is no less the father's than the other—the real question the child has to answer is not which one is metaphysically true, but which one he himself is going to allow to be the governing word in the relationship. In short, he has to decide only this: when push comes to shove, *which word is he personally going to allow to matter most?*

We're slow to do that, of course, both with our own fathers' as well as the Father's words. And for some strange reason, when we do decide it, we often make the most of the least comforting word we can find. I have often thought that maybe God isn't any happier about his Fathering than we are about ours. After all the centuries of exploding and yelling at us (necessarily, for we are dense)—after all those lectures about what really is best—he finally gave, as his last Word on the subject, a Savior who said, "Father, forgive them." He has, in other words, said, "It's all right." Unfortunately for us, and no doubt exasperatingly for him, we can hardly bring ourselves to believe it.

That's a desperate situation, but not a serious one. It can be remedied simply by remembering that everything he's said to us is a father's word. It will always contain more than we want to hear because he wants from us—for our own good—more than we care to produce. But by the same token, it will always end with the assurance that he wants *us* most of all—that, as far as he is concerned, he isn't going to make our unproductiveness an obstacle to his wants.

Accordingly, I feel myself free, in the instant case of the Father's Word on remarriage and adultery, to take all of his assertions at full force. I find it quite unnecessary to get myself off the hook by arguing that Jesus was using oriental hyperbole (he didn't *really* mean remarried divorcées were adulterers, any more than he meant for the offending eye to be literally plucked out), or by attempting any other attenuation of his remarks. Instead, I read Scripture and note that Jesus identifies three species of adultery: the common garden, or slipping-between-the-sheets-on-the-side variety; the peeking piker, or Whosoever-Looketh-Upon-A-Woman-To-Lust-After-Her type; and the remarital, or don't-think-it's-cheap-to-break-promises mode. Next, I look at my own life and find that I have, as it were, scored in all three categories. In life as in golf, though, less would have been more: I was supposed to be breaking a hundred on the way down, not up. Finally, therefore, I conclude that I am, by the Father's Word, a sinner.

Three things need to be said about that. The first is that it's hardly news. In spite of the prurient custom of counting sexual sins twice and other kinds hardly at all, the fact remains that by any honest count I am not now, nor have I ever been, a nonsinner. I have lied when it suited my convenience, been mean when I was in the mood, loafed when I could get away with it and, in general, thrown myself manfully into the endless struggle to think well of myself. If adultery is one more particular in that list, all it means is that the Pharisee's speech ("My God, I thank thee that I am not as other men are: adulterers, unjust . . .) is obviously not for me. If I stand before my Father at all, it will have to be on the Publican's terms; "God, be merciful to me, a sinner."

Which leads me to the second point. Not only is my sinfulness not news; it is especially not good news. It may be that deep in my nature there is a circuit missing, but I have never been able to understand the glee the world derives from pointing out the existence of sin. Most sins are no fun for anybody (jealousy wreathes no faces in smiles; anger causes a frown line for every point it makes); and the few that have attendant pleasures cause so many hangups and hangovers that they're hardly worth the price of hanging in. To talk about the subject as if it were exciting is worse than cheering for crabgrass.

There is, of course, good news all around the fringes of sin, but oddly, the world is indisposed to pay much attention to it. The church, in her wisdom, has always known the almost perverse gladness of the Gospel: "Sin is behovely," said the Lady Julian, "and all shall be well, and all shall be well, and all manner of thing shall be well." And on Easter Eve, the faithful look back on Adam's muffing of the ball and sing "O happy fault . . ." But on the other hand, the church in her stupidity (she has a treasury of that, too) forgets about forgiveness with alarming regularity.

So much so that not only the world, but even her members believe more easily in the Godfather than in God the Father. For me, though, the Word in which I ultimately believe (not because I can prove it's true, but simply because I have decided to let it govern my thinking) is not in Sicilian. It is that the Lamb of God who took away the sins of the world used a shovel, not a sifter. He got all of them, not just some. There are lots of things we shouldn't do, but there isn't one of them we can't have done and still come home. We sure as hell may not be able to get permission for a damned thing. But if there's a heaven, that's all beside the point. Forgiveness is the last word on everything.

I talk to people. Like the woman who had an abortion years ago and never forgave herself. People tried to persuade her, she told me, that taking a life like that wasn't wrong. She was never convinced. Could I help her?

To do what, I asked? To come to some advanced level of moral theology at which sin x could be proved nonsinful? Or to arrive at some pitch of personal perfection that would insure her never doing anything wrong again?

If it was the first, I told her, forget it. Moral theology is like trying to push down laundry in a washtub: for every item you manage to sink out of sight, two more pop up at you. And if it was the second, all I could say was, fat chance. Why didn't she just decide to trust God's Word that she was forgiven?

She said she would like that but she couldn't feel it. I answered that she didn't have to feel it, only to decide to trust it. She said she found it just unbelievable. I said it wasn't that at all: it might be unknowable, unimaginable or even unacceptable to her; but it was precisely and only believable. How come, when she had a choice of the kind of news she could believe in, she picked bad news instead of good?

Look, I said. When she was in church, she sang, "Lamb of God, you take away the sins of the world; have mercy on us." Where does it say which ones he didn't take? What did she want the choir to do, insert a list before the semicolon and sing: ". . . except for Martha's abortion on demand and Robert's adulteries any style"?

I can't, I told her, prove that such exceptions shouldn't be in there. For all I know, the only reason they aren't is that they would mess up the music. But since they aren't, I consider the omission a piece of personal good luck and skip all the questions to which I couldn't stand the answers anyway. Anybody tells me good news, I listen.

But, she said, aren't sins still wrong? Isn't it kind of outrageous just to be able to walk up and get forgiveness for something you could never have gotten permission for? Mightn't people take advantage of a situation like that?

I told her, Yes. Yes, and Yes. But since the risk was all God's and not hers, why didn't she leave the question of whether he was operating on a sound business basis to the theological actuaries and just enjoy the free assurance?

"But the church . . ." she said. "Doesn't Christianity

have an obligation to uphold the moral law? What if . . ."

At that point, fortunately, Madeleine appeared grinning in the doorway with three bottles of Beck's and warbled, "Free beer, anyone?" The moment of exasperation passed. Our friend even stayed for supper.

However, since I didn't get a chance to deliver my final answer to her, I shall give it to you now as this long, slow curve makes its low and possibly outside way across the plate.

"But the church . . ." she said.

Butt the church. And butt the obligation of Christians to be a cheering section for the Ten Commandments. Everybody has an obligation to uphold the moral law—and the assorted armies of righteousness, secular as well as religious, do very well by it: they not only beat up on transgressors, they also do a fair job of fomenting wars with each other. What the dear old thickheaded church has a primary obligation to proclaim is forgiveness—a message that is simply obscured when she acts as if "Thou shalt not commit . . . whatever," is big news.

Butt her hard, therefore. And butt her over and over until she wakes up and realizes that she is not some kind of club for the well behaved, or a self-improvement school for the improvable, or even a society for turning human beings into Christians. She is none of those. She is simply the sign to the world of the great, gray-green, greasy good news that God has lost his picky taste for such gourmet spiritual recipes and acquired a vulgar, catholic one for forgiveness.

The whole, damned world is home free. Every word of that is true; but only two of them make it nice. Why on earth is it so hard to decide which?

XVII

REMARRIAGE & REFORM

One more small job and we can go back and sit by the stove. I promised you something oriental for dinner, so I'd better get the meats out of the freezer now: some ground pork, I think, and a small steak, plus a couple of chicken breasts.

What are we having? Well, Madeleine and I lived in New York City for a few months before we came here, and we've been addicts of Thai cooking ever since. We found ourselves in Queens, in the neighborhood I grew up in. But over the years since my boyhood its original WASP-Irish population had been pretty well supplanted by succeeding layers of immigrants. It began with South Americans, who gave the place its first new wave of cookery since it was settled. When I was a child, I came up the block after school to the smell of liver and onions; now it's tripe with *chorizos* and *morcillas* with rice and beans. People don't always eat at home, of course; as before, they still go out to Chinese restaurants. But the menus are now in Spanish, and the Chinese cooks are from Cuba and the prices . . . well, China-Latina food is one of New York's few remaining bargains.

But to the point. The second wave of ethnic cookery to hit the neighborhood was Thai-Vietnamese. Thai restaurants have sprung up all over the city since then, and the cuisine has become fashionable and therefore expensive. But when we were there, we had the pleasure of discovering it all on our own—and without having to pay for chic. For two months we ate out three nights a week, working our way through the menu of a neighborhood Thai restaurant with only eight tables. On the off nights, I'd go to the Thai grocery across the street, ask all the questions I could think of, buy the ingredients I needed and go home and try to imitate the previous night's dishes.

Tonight you get three of them: Chicken in coconut milk with *galanga*; a *Yam*, or salad, of sliced steak with greens, red onion, coriander, mint, basil, lime juice, red pepper, fish sauce, lemon grass and garlic; and something called *Nam Sod*, or ground pork and peanuts with similar oddments and even more chili peppers. Hot and fragrant. You'll love it. It's positively habit-forming.

What's that? Do I always have things like ground pork and chicken breasts in the freezer? Oh, my, yes. What I do is wait till whole chickens are forty-nine cents a pound —or whole pork loins, seventy-nine cents; then I break them down to my own specifications and freeze the results. Just from two big (twenty-four-pound) loins, for instance, I've got a freezer well stocked with a couple of small roasts, packages of chops, bags of boneless chunks for oriental dishes, three kinds of homemade sausage in bulk (Italian, *chorizo*, breakfast), plain ground pork and (from the bones and trimmings) scrapple. That last, in fact, suggests a solution to the problem of tomorrow's meal. I think I'll fetch rather a lot of it and make us a real down-home Sunday brunch: scrapple, sausage, bacon, eggs, hash-browns. . . . My kitchen now may be heavily oriental, but as you can see, it's not dogmatically so. Mostly, I'm just a cook from way back who also enjoys being far out. The cuisine has undergone lots of changes over the years, but I just go right on rattling the pots and pans.

It makes you wonder, doesn't it, how much we ourselves really change? True enough, when you get divorced and remarried, you feel as if nothing in your life has been left in its old place. But after a while, you begin to realize that the great upheaval may not have produced as many differences in you as you thought. In particular, I note that the number of them you can chalk up under the heading of general self-improvement tends to be surprisingly, even discouragingly small.

Not that there aren't changes. It's just that we over-estimate the role of our own willpower in causing them. We live in an age of self-improvement schemes: if you buy the right book or follow the right regimen, you're guaranteed to achieve a perfect figure, terrific sex and a heart like an ox—or confidence, wisdom, serenity and the ability to get your own way without being unpopular. And sure enough, the occasional vice does go obligingly down the drain and the odd virtue shoots up where it never grew before.

But there are two things that need to be said about that basically navel-watching approach to life. The first is that it's based on an unwarrantedly optimistic view of human nature. It assumes that we have it in our power to change our lives, and that all that's needed to convert our history from disaster to triumph is a new diet, better advice or the right religion. It leads us to think, in other words, that the years of our lives not only should, but actually can succeed each other in a kind of progressive elimination of what's wrong with us. You know: this year you'll conquer smoking, next year, worry, the year after that, insecurity—all on the underlying assumption that you are the master of your fate and that if you live long enough, you can turn yourself into a perfect peach.

I don't know about you, but as far as I'm concerned, my life not only hasn't worked that way, but isn't about to, either. If it's been peachy (and it has been, more often than I had any right to expect), it still has plenty of rust marks and squishy spots that show no signs of responding to deliberate treatment. The day of my death, no matter how long it tarries, shows little promise of being the grand climax of a history of self-improvement. If I don't die of my faults, I will nevertheless die with them. The likelihood of their predeceasing me is pretty slim.

That's not a gloomy view, however. It doesn't mean there can't be changes in my ways; only that they'll come, when they do, in response to some other force than my own willpower. At least the big ones will—and that brings me to the second thing that needs saying.

The removal of major aberrations from our lives is almost always not our handiwork; it's simply a gift dropped into our laps. The most convenient illustration of that truth is probably AA. It begins by insisting not that its members conquer their problem, but that they admit they are in fact powerless to do anything about it. And it proceeds, by a gift of attention and concern, to provide a new context in which the old, unconquered problem simply does not arise as it once did.

A less convenient, but nonetheless handier illustration of the same truth is the quite unplanned (by me, at any rate) disappearance from my life of the fairly energetic habit of adultery I pursued over a number of years. One is not, especially if one is a priest, supposed to talk about such things—at least the guardians of uprightness don't smile too broadly when you do. Of the four areas in which the clergy habitually undistinguish themselves—intellectual error, alcoholic excess, homosexual indulgence and heterosexual trespass (conveniently memorable as the four B's: books, booze, boys and broads)—the church has been able to find only the subjects of books and booze even slightly fit for airing. The final two remain quite firmly stuffed in the closet—with the last one, if anything, further back than the third.

Still, why not talk? Not about the details, of course. That's simply bad manners—something that gentlemen and ladies don't do, even if . . . Especially if. But to say nothing at all about it is to miss not only the chance to talk about something the authorities haven't yet been able to water down from a sin into a sickness, but also the pleasure of seeing how grace actually works.

The habit of adultery, as I said, simply disappeared. But not as the result of a successful campaign on my part to extirpate it; rather as a result of Madeleine's presence in my life. And not because she either asked for or insisted on reform. It went away because she took—and takes up—so much room that it just had no more place. One doesn't conquer adultery by moral teeth clenching any more than one ends the years of masturbation by resolution. The only accurate description of the way any essentially narcissistic habit is broken is that somebody finally comes along with such a huge and surprising gift that you simply forget to look at yourself.

Where I would be without that gift is an interesting, if not an important question. Probably the best answer to it is to parallel the AA formula: I have not become a nonadulterer, any more than an AA member becomes a nonalcoholic. I'm just somewhere, by gift and by design, where the subject, as it once was, doesn't come up. What matters is not that I can cook up some claim that I've improved, but that I have known the working of grace. Even if I were to lapse back into the old narcissistic habit, I would still know now the only way its grip can be broken.

What I find most comforting about all that is how close it lies to the actual biblical teaching about Sin and Grace. Sin is not the same as sins—at least not as they're commonly conceived: as vices, as naughty things that shouldn't be done. Sin is a preoccupation with one's self; and its opposite is not virtue, but faith: the abandonment of one's self, in trust, to somebody else. That's why, even though I have quite freely confessed to adultery (and lots of other *sins*) my real repentance over my history does not extend to saying bad things about my past. There were some genuine, even monumental love affairs there; my deepest sorrow is over the way self-preoccupation did them in along with so much else.

Even at that, though, Sin isn't the only inconvenience in life. Grace makes just as much trouble. My marriage ended, I think, not because of the affairs—all of them, in fact, were turned off before it was—but because of the same gift that did them in: Madeleine's propensity for taking up room. And if that doesn't sound like the world's most upstanding state of affairs, marital or otherwise, at least I haven't faked too much of it in the telling: some of my vices disappeared in the onslaught of grace; so did a good bit of my virtue. It just underscores the fact that I shouldn't try to make either of them into an article of standing or falling for myself.

It proves, in fact, my old point: we don't play very well in the angelic leagues. Marriage, Romance, Remarriage—the gorgeous angels we so gladly invite to rule over us—all have in their pockets lists of the changes we need to make in our lives before they can be happy with us; unfortunately, the lists are all different and the changes are mostly out of our hands. Better we should just settle for the inconvenience of grace.

No doubt someone will read this and cluck about the fact that I don't seem to believe in anything anymore—not even in trying to do the right thing. That's nonsense. All I'm saying is that since the angels have always had me in a losing battle—and since I seem chronically indisposed to getting off the field—I'd rather take my chances in my own skin than suit up in their armor. Right along with everybody else, I'm going to go on believing in all sorts of wonderful stuff and trying to do what I can to achieve it. But I'm not, for all that, going to lose sleep over what the angels think of my performance. Once again: if God has said, "It's all right," that's that. Not to believe it would be the biggest nonsense of all.

XVIII

REMARRIAGE &
RETHINKING

Nevertheless, if you feel constrained to press me a little harder on the subject of change, I can't say I blame you. Haven't there been, you want to ask me, more changes in my life than I'm willing to admit to? Do I really think that the only substantial difference between the way I was and the way I am is that now forgiveness is more important to me than angelic approval? What about self-approval? I seem content in the extreme. Could it be that, unbeknownst to myself, I have conformed to higher standards—or have I perhaps, it occurs to you darkly, achieved my satisfaction by adopting less exalted ones? I tripped the first time over the matrimonial high jump. Maybe I'm only making it this time because I've lowered the bar.

Let me dispose of your question about self-approval first. To me, the subject is a nonsubject, at least as far as flesh and blood are concerned. Human beings don't need to mess with it from one end of their days to the other. When they are right, or good, or healthy or wise, they will automatically enjoy their lives without having to send themselves telegrams of congratulation. And when they are not, all such narcissistic backslapping is fakery to begin with. What they need therefore is not self-approval, but the sense to get rid of self-disapproval by the only device that works: accepting somebody else's approval and dropping the whole subject. The Prodigal, once he's home, doesn't need to speak well of his unspeakable self; he just enjoys the party his Father's acceptance offers him. It's the Elder Brother, with his list of self-endorsements, who spends the miserable afternoon. Self-approval be damned then. It's nothing but angelic approval in disguise and it poops every human party it's allowed near.

Your next question, however, cannot be answered so flatly. You suggest that perhaps I am being excessively modest, or cagey—that maybe I really have changed for the better but am hedging bets on my happiness by refusing to talk about it. I have two thoughts about that. The first is that if I have, I have, but yammering about it on my part isn't going to contribute a thing to my enjoyment. As I said, so little of it is my own doing that it ill behooves me to take time out from thanking others to chronicle the developments.

But the second is to insist that it isn't for me to say whether I've changed or not. For one thing, I still believe, with Jeremiah, that "the heart is deceitful above all things, and desperately wicked." When someone gives you his opinion, pro or contra, of himself, the chances of its being anything but a con job are minuscule. For another, I receive such regular and varied intelligence on the subject of the changes I think I have attempted (that they have been for the better, or for the worse or simply undetectable) that I really have no idea what to say other than to refer you to my sources. Ask Madeleine, or my children, or my first wife or the ecclesiastical authorities, if you like. Their opinions make quite a tapestry; but since I haven't figured out even whether I'm looking at the front or the back, you may as well examine it yourself.

But as to your major question—which, in plain English, is whether I have contented myself in remarriage by watering down the whole idea of marriage—I feel I owe you something more than just disallowing it or disqualifying myself. Let me start therefore with what is perhaps not quite so plain an answer and work my way along from there.

As I see it, any revisions I have made in my thinking about marriage have involved not so much changes in the substance of what I believe, as alterations in the angle from which I choose to come at it. That's no doubt due to having spent so many years teaching dogmatic theology. In spite of its shirty-sounding name, it's actually one of the most liberating disciplines in the world. The only stricture it lays upon its practitioners is that they may not sweep any pieces of the received faith under the rug. Short of that, though, it leaves them free to do almost anything they can with them. A theologian, for instance, may formulate a dozen doctrines of Hell: he may make it so odd a prospect that, conceivably, no one will be in it, or so severe a one that nearly everybody is. The one thing he is not allowed to do, though, is omit the treatise *On Hell* from his work.

In that, his approach is no different from the one I described a while back in connection with Holy Scripture (it's all the Word of God: pick it up any way you like, but don't refuse to pick any of it up). It is also very much like the attitude of the experimental scientist: he may revise his theories every day in the week, but on no day is he allowed to fudge a fact.

Applied to marriage, that attitude leads me to accept lock, stock and barrel all the old ordonnance which the church has fired off on the subject: the apparently safe items, like loving, honoring and cherishing for better or for worse, in sickness and in health; but also the (to the remarried) explosive ones like staying married till death do us part. I do not expect, of course, that you or anyone else will necessarily think well of the style in which I pick up the various pieces. But since I do pick them all up, we are at least talking about the same subjects.

By way of a first illustration, therefore, let me comment on the phrase "forsaking all others" that occurs in the received text of almost everybody's marriage rite. Obviously, if it is taken as prescriptive law—as enunciating a requirement which, if broken, renders us clean contrary to the whole idea of marriage—then it is not simply a hard saying for the remarried; it is something that renders second marriages ipso facto illegal. Your second wife is just one more other you should have forsaken in the name of your first; under that rubric, your union with her has no status at all.

However, if the phrase is picked up as a description rather than a prescription, it becomes not only easier to handle, but also more accessible to the remarried. Suppose, by way of analogy, that you give your child a car on his eighteenth birthday. Among other things, you tell him that he must keep the air and oil filters clean. If that is taken as a prescriptive law, both of you will be led down inconvenient byways. You, having promulgated the law, will be tempted to take the car back in punishment for his failure to observe your prescription. He, on the other hand, when the prescription irks him, will simply ignore it as having importance only to you.

The danger in that is obvious if you press the analogy further. Suppose, having been deprived by you of his first car because he broke the law, he nevertheless acquires a second quite on his own. You know, and I know, that the rule about filters is really a descriptive law: it enunciates not what your son must do to make himself acceptable to you, but the procedure he must follow if he wants to have a car that works. Punishment, if we can call it that, is not something imposed by the lawgiver; it is meted out by the nature of the thing the law was about. But if he does not know that—if he goes on seeing the rule as your prescription only and not as rooted in the nature of the car—he sets himself up for a lifetime of ruined engines.

Turn that around now and apply it to "forsaking all others." Taken as a prescriptive law, it simply mires people in a contractual obligation to do certain defined acts only with their spouses; when and if they happen to do them with others, their minds focus chiefly and inevitably on their own status as contract breakers. But not only does that distract them from what the law was about; it also leads them to the dangerous conclusion that, having broken the law, they no longer have any meaningful connection with it. If, however, it's simply a description of how human relationships in fact work, that conclusion is not necessary at all. It doesn't matter how many marriages you've ruined by not paying sufficient attention to the rule: it goes right on being true, and you'll never get any marriage to run right until you learn to heed it.

Something more needs to be added, however. Besides being a descriptive rather than a prescriptive law of relationships, it is also a special kind of description. "Keep your filters clean" is straightforward instruction; it can and was meant to be followed literally. But "forsaking all others" is hyperbole. It refers not to a literal withdrawal from everyone but your spouse, but to the unique and intense kind of attention you need to pay if you want to continue to have a spouse at all. It doesn't mean that all inattention is forbidden (else how would you watch even a bowl game on TV); nor, in particular, does it mean that there are certain supreme inattentions (for example, adultery) that are necessarily more lethal than others. It simply means that below a rather high level of personal attentiveness, trouble will inevitably brew.

"Forsaking all others," therefore, is a kind of dramatic shorthand for such attentiveness. It can, of course, be seen as applying to almost any literal forsaking we may choose; and conversely, if we were to let it apply to none, it would end up with no meaning whatsoever. But for all that, its literal sense can never exhaust its meaning. In short, it is precisely hyperbolical truth: not mere hyperbole and not mere truth, but both, inseparably wrapped together in one package. It's a perfect parallel to "If a man smite you on the cheek, turn to him the other also": you might on one day take that to mean just what it says, and on another to mean only that you should suffer through the second half of his boring monologue. In either case, the fundamental meaning is plain enough: it's that the business of staying in relationships with others calls for an extravagant gift of openness on your part. Whether it's putting up with oppression or paying attention, if you have to ask the price, you can't afford it.

As I said, if you feel that's a cavalier way to deal with a received text, feel free to sit loose. At the very least, it's a way that does deal with it, and it sounds a warning about the dangers of making prescriptive (or even descriptive) laws out of hyperbolical statements. Still, let me give you another illustration that goes a bit further in the same vein: my reflections on the assertion that when two people marry, they become "one flesh." Once again, it's a doctrine that hangs menacingly over remarried heads. Let's see if it can't be rethought rather than removed.

Plainly, all the strictures already laid down about not making prescriptions out of descriptions apply here. For no matter how often in history the notion of "one flesh" has been made the basis of legalisms, none of them has been particularly convincing. If it was taken as a literal truth, for example, it weighed as much against remarriage after widowhood as after divorce. Accordingly, rather arbitrary adjustments had to be made: widows might remarry on the grounds that death put an end to the flesh; the divorced might not because in their case, only the oneness was brought to an end—and by a mere decision at that. The fact that in the second case the "one flesh" had been abrogated just as really as in the first was not allowed into consideration. The sword of the law, however, once taken up, is hard to put down: some remarriages of people with living spouses were eventually allowed. Annulments, for example, were granted on the argument that even though the flesh of the marriage was still around, there had been something missing (consent, willingness to have children) in the oneness department; therefore, all appearances to the contrary, there never had been one flesh in the first place.

But all that simply goes to show the unreality of trying to make laws out of the wrong material. If the hyperbole of "forsaking all others" made it an unsuitable basis for legislation, much more did the metaphor involved in "one flesh" make for questionable morality. For it is precisely a metaphor, not a literal statement of fact: it takes the unity of a living body and uses it as an icon of marriage. It is an image, a parable: we get truth from it not by squeezing legalisms out of (or into) the details of its parts, but by holding up the whole as a mirror to reality.

You don't, in other words, set yourself the job of deciding whether marriages are valid on the basis of some definable notion of oneness or fleshness. (Think, if you will, of all the knots people tied themselves into over that enterprise: having to finagle the marriage of the Blessed Virgin and Saint Joseph into validity even though it was short on the flesh; having to deny the marriage of a man who sat on a hand grenade, for the same reason; inventing ways of disqualifying obviously fleshly unions for lack of theoretical oneness.) What you do instead is say simply: "one flesh" is an image of what marriage is like when it's most like itself. Instead of turning it into a requirement, you allow it to be a reflection.

But obviously, since it's an ideal, not an actual reflection, it can and often will stand in contrast to the marriages we hold up to it. Equally obviously, there will be things—some of them uncomfortably instructive things— that we can learn from our looking at it. But to use it as a device for deciding whether a particular marriage can stand in front of the mirror at all is just foolishness.

Therefore, when I think about "one flesh" in the context of remarriage, I do so not to find out whether I'm legal, but to learn the name of the game I am, and always have been, playing. It does not inform me that, having popped out on my one and only allowable swing at the flesh, I can't play any more; it says that no matter how often I get up at bat—and regardless of whether I hit, walk or strike out—the game of which marriage is the sacrament isn't going to be canceled for anything. Precisely because I am flesh, the ball of oneness—even if I miss it—is still in play.

For if marriage is the sacrament—the effective sign, the real presence—of the oneness for which all flesh was created, then it's not only silly but dangerous to talk about it as if it were the only instance in which that oneness can have meaning. It's like *confining* Christ's presence to the Bread and Wine of Communion, rather than seeing them as signs of his unconfined presence everywhere—like taking a universal mystery we were supposed to recognize as carrying us and turning it into a particular gesture by which we have to get ourselves on board.

And if I'm unwilling to allow that to happen to the "oneness" aspect of the metaphor, I'm even less willing to do it as far as the "flesh" is concerned. I will not force it to be the basis for any particular requirement or restriction. My first wife was the sign to me of our common humanity. And she still is, just as I am to her. And so is Madeleine. It strikes me as supremely unimportant to try to reduce the meaning of those sacramental experiences to a question of who is currently eating or sleeping with whom. What matters is not whether we achieved some recognizable standard of oneness (we did and we didn't, in both cases); but whether we ourselves recognize that precisely because we are flesh, the way to oneness is always open. Unlike the angels, we can always forgive and be forgiven. They may have to keep the warfare in the heavenly bookkeeping department going forever; we can simply tell each other in truth, "That's all right," and by that absolution let the one flesh we inevitably are matter more than all the angelic harmony we never achieved.

That does not, of course, come cheap. In the process, we can and will have to do two more things that the flesh is heir to: suffer and die. But it is just those fleshly possibilities, it seems to me, that are the deepest and most dependable root of our oneness. The unions we have enjoyed, mostly by dumb luck—and the ones we have shipwrecked by unlucky dumbness—all skate on the surface of a oneness that breaks upwards into our humanity every time we stop letting the angels tell us that we have to survive. It is quite safe for us to get ourselves out of the way. In fact, when it comes to oneness, we're the biggest thing that's in the way.

To anyone who learned that lesson in a first and only

marriage, I offer my heartfelt—and totally unnecessary—congratulations: you know what you have. But to anyone who didn't, and who is now in another marriage trying to learn it for the first time, I offer something more cheering still: you've already got it; and the minute you settle for being only and forgivingly mortal, you'll know it.

What you have to do to hear the music is shut off your own noise.

XIX

REMARRIAGE &
NEW PATTERNS

You see now, perhaps, the reason for my antsiness about either claiming credit or accepting blame for possible changes in my life—for my reluctance, in fact, to allow the subject even the houseroom I have given it. Having been involved for so many years with the angels, I have simply had my fill of trying to run my life according to my own, or anybody else's, bright ideas. If I have learned anything through the lengthening second day that is my remarriage, it's that there are no recipes for mixing up a batch of life—none, at least, that are proof against the kind of foolishness I so regularly bring to the job.

Hence my enthusiasm for my admittedly odd interpretation of "one flesh." It strikes me that what we most need is not the questionable assurance of good advice (we had that and now stand only condemned by it), but the ability to trust that if we will just confine ourselves to being merely human, something far deeper than our own plans and contrivances will carry us. It's the flesh, not the soul or the mind, that is the engine of salvation.

How do I arrive at that conclusion? By two routes, one negative, the other positive. On the minus side, I note that the major mischiefs human beings make are rooted not in the fact that they're flesh, but in their inveterate attempts to be something more refined than that. It's precisely in the name of the good, the better and the best that we most often beat up on one another. Wars are fought for noble causes and righteous reasons; families are torn apart not by the weakness of the mortal bodies that comprise them, but by the reckless eagerness of the spirits involved to transcend infirmity. I have always—and so have you—done far more damage by insisting on rightness than I ever did by being wrong. Wrongness is at least amenable to forgiveness. People who are right are amenable to nothing.

But it's the positive route that puts the note of hope in the conclusion. When God decided it was time to save the world, he did so by being only and totally human. After all the millennia of angelic jawboning about righteousness, he shut up and died like a man to the whole subject. I'm aware that that's not the usual view of what he did. The church has all too often gone right on giving everyone the impression that correctness is still the linchpin of the universe. But it seems to me that in the silence of what he finally did, he put an end to all that noise: he made good on his totally unheavenly promise to remember our sins and our iniquities no more. The subject was killing us, so he just dropped it. And he told us to deal with it the same way: go ahead and die, so we can get rid of it too.

That, of course, will inevitably sound to you like a religious truth, and a specifically Christian one besides. All I can say is that it no longer sounds like that to me. It may have been revealed in the course of religious history, and its proclamation may have been committed to a particular ecclesiastical entity; but for all that, I find it not a religious truth but a cosmic one. It is the announcement that we are going to be set to rights not by structured actions which only some of us will ever manage, but by coming unstructured in a passion that all of us will inevitably undergo. If we die, we shall live. The flesh at its most fleshly is our hope.

And that is what makes the hope a catholic and not a sectarian one. The "if" in "if we die" refers not to a possible option but to a certain development. It means "when" or "as soon as." It tells us that the reconciliation of all our relationships is not only inevitably in the works by the very fact of our humanity—by our final death, *when* we die; but also that the reconciliation is enjoyable in the present every time we stop trying to fake out our humanity—through our many lesser deaths, *as soon as we* are willing to die them. Our restoration is not a reward for finally getting our act together; it's simply the result of letting it fall apart fruitfully. The seed goes safely into the ground to die. Its deepest business is already built into its mortal nature; happily, therefore, all the rest is simply not its business.

As I said, that's a belief, not a piece of verifiable information. But since it is so much better news than anything else I have ever heard—and since there isn't anyone to whom it could possibly be worse news than what he already knows—I find it's the only news I'm interested in giving out. When people come to me now to talk about remarriage, or even marriage, I have almost nothing else to say. Not that there aren't, as there always were, plenty of prudent words I could give them; it's just that telling them it's all right to let themselves be done in seems to be the only hopeful word. Advice, they can always fail to take. What they need most is the confidence that it's safe to fail.

Therefore, what I now have to say to those who are remarrying boils down to one warning and one illustration. They come to me, of course, on the crest of a new wave in their lives—at the beginning of what they see as a second chance, a second life, a second day. And they speak (even the ones to whose background the category is alien) about resurrection, about how they finally feel alive from the dead again.

We drink a glass of wine to that; throwing cold water on enthusiasm is not my style. But then I caution them about their arithmetic. Resurrection, I tell them, comes on the third day, and it's something over which they have no control at all. They didn't cause the one they're now enjoying, as they perfectly well know. If they caused anything, it was just the deaths out of which they rose. But, by that same token, they cannot, by aiming at resurrection, keep it going. Their real job, therefore, in this second day of their lives is what the work of the second day always is: staying dead enough so resurrection can happen.

They got to where they now are, I remind them, out of deaths. Unimaginably, the worst thing that ever happened to them has turned out to be the best thing that ever happened for them. What they must guard against now is losing sight of how it worked and lapsing back into trying simply to keep themselves alive. They have not only seen the universal truth that life comes out of death, they are positively enjoying it: therefore, don't blow it by balking at death. It's perfectly safe to throw your life away. In fact, it's the only condition of getting it back.

Since, however, it's easy to balk at the exalted generality of that, I go on to insist that I mean something quite

pedestrian and specific by it. All I'm telling them is to let
the grand shipwreck out of which they have been resur-
rected make them bold enough not to be afraid of the
little ones that will happen every day. They should forget
about saving their egos, or their ideas, or their indepen-
dence or their prerogatives. Every time either of them gets
a chance, he should kill off such efforts at cautious living
and just be dead so that resurrection will have a chance.

That, of course, usually forces an objection out of them.
Do I really mean for people just to make themselves into
doormats for each other? Couldn't that reduce your identity to zero? Well, I say to them, as far as I can see, my
identity came out of nothing to begin with, and will
come back up out of nothing to end with, so why should
I balk about a few more exposures to the condition in
between—especially since my efforts at being somebody
have not exactly been a howling success?

But, they want to know, isn't that risky? Suppose the
person you're married to just takes advantage of all that
self-effacement? Where are you then?

I point out to them that they know perfectly well where
they are then: they're in a bad marriage. But since they've
been there before and risen out of it, so what? What's
more important is that they should consider the alternative to self-effacement—which is: angelic self-assertion es-
calated into a war that nobody can win because nobody's
willing to be human enough to lose. Sure, if you make a
habit of giving in trustingly to your partner, you could
very well be taken advantage of. But there are two things
to be said about that. The first is that if your trust is misplaced, you'll soon enough find that out by the fact that
your partner hasn't the least interest in giving in to you.
And that will kill you. And that, in turn, will take you
back to the master condition of your life, namely, being

dead. At which point (unless you've forgotten how you got there in the first place), you are back to start and ready to rise.

But if your trust is not misplaced—if your partner really is willing to shed his ego, at least occasionally, for your sake—what will you do by angelically hanging on to yours except discourage him on more and more occasions? True enough, that too can only kill you and send you back to start. But why wait so long and unhappily to get there when you could have been dying and rising all along?

It's the pattern of little deaths, therefore, that contributes most to the pattern of continuing resurrection. And, to provide a properly minor illustration of that major truth, I give them the historical background of two watchwords Madeleine and I have developed to remind ourselves of it.

One day, by a switch of our already switched roles, she was cutting up celery for egg salad and I was sitting in the kitchen. Her method of dicing was as follows: take a stalk of celery, slice it lengthwise with a paring knife, turn it, slice it crosswise; take another stalk of celery . . . etc., all in leisurely, if not slow motion. My method, which is more than three times as fast, is to chop the stalks lengthwise with a Chinese cleaver all at once, then turn them and do the same crosswise. I suggested, therefore, in the midst of her operation, that she would do better to adopt at least part of my approach and wait until all the lengthwise cuts were made so she could do the crosscutting in volume.

Her reaction was to slam the knife down on the board and march out of the room, throwing watchword number one over her shoulder:

"If you're not doing it, don't!"

Comment

I leave to our own knowledge of that day's history—and to your fertile psychological guesswork about our relationship—the precise details of what preceded that outburst. Suffice it to say that she had had more than one day's exposure to my chronic self-importance and, when she finally spotted the chance I missed to tell myself to drop dead and shut up, she did it for me.

Had I done so, the illustration would have been more minor still, and the death involved, practically minimal. But I do not think I have to tell you how much extended dying the failure to offer it to her produced. Before we got to a fruitful death, we ran a gamut of grievances produced mostly by my compulsive belief that my identity should be free to obtrude itself, night and day, on other people's lives: on the way they drove cars, on the way they reasoned, on the way they felt, on the way, in short, they were. Luckily, we finally did get there; but how much better it would have been—and is now, when I'm not afraid to let my two cents' worth of identity get lost—to say to myself, "If you're not doing it, don't!" and simply shut up.

The second watchword came out of a situation just the reverse of that.

It is my habit to cook the evening meal. When Madeleine and I were first together, in fact, it was also my pleasure to do everything connected with it, from setting the table to cleaning up. Bit by bit, though, the availability of help (Madeleine's, or children's) in those adjunct tasks led my large but less than energetic ego to divorce itself from them. After that, it was only a short walk to the position that my identity was somehow threatened if no one else did them for me. And from there, only a step to self-pitying fury that I was being trampled on if I was not being helped.

I steamed about that for longer than I like to remember and, in the process, gave off a good many vibrations that had little in common with the risen life. But then one day I thought back to the time when I had done the whole job gladly, and I came up, on my own, with our second ego-killing phrase:

"If you are doing it, do it all!"

Comment

If the first watchword is the death of the identity that has to impose itself, this one is a mortal blow to the self that takes pity at its being imposed upon. It applies all across the board: to getting somebody else to make your phone calls, balance your books or correct your children; to promising to help your partner and then doing only half the job on the grounds that it's not your job; to making, in short, your two cents' worth conditional on somebody else's one-cent contribution.

Neglect it, and you leave a nasty, half-living ego around to produce resentment in yourself and a pain in the neck in others. Observe it, and in the death of that obnoxious self, you find a giver of gifts who is welcome to all.

What both watchwords say, then, is what I've been getting at all along: the great advantage flesh has over the angels is that it's disposable and they aren't—and that it's precisely in being at the disposal of others that we conform ourselves to the pattern that takes away the indispositions of the world.

XX

THE NEWEST PATTERN

Which reminds me. If we're going to have bread to dispose of properly when Madeleine gets back, we should go out to the kitchen and see how the loaves are progressing. Overproofing is as much of a mistake as underproofing, so join me once again, if you will. I realize you must feel like an ambulatory delegate to a bakers' union convention, but bear with me and you shall have a respite. When we get the bread out and the wine poured, I promise to stop nattering till after supper. I may not have too many virtues, but one of them is that I never pontificate once the cocktail hour has started.

That, incidentally, is a principle with me that's even stronger than my religion. A number of years ago, when the church took up the vogue of scheduling a Sunday Mass for 5 P.M. on Saturdays, some parishioners of mine asked me if I was going to go along. The idea was simply inconceivable to me, but since they kept coming up with all sorts of practical reasons for it, I felt I owed them a theoretical justification of my flat refusal. Finally I came up with it. "If God had meant us to have evening Masses," I told them, "he would have put the cocktail hour somewhere else." There's nothing like sound theology for collapsing a ballooning inconvenience.

But as you can see, these loaves will collapse if we give them much more proofing, so let me heat up the oven and fetch the razor. Meanwhile, if you'll put these baking sheets gently on the counter . . .

There. Painless. We are back at the living room stove again and, while the bread bakes, I think I shall give you one last helping—if it is that—of explanation. You were patient when I discoursed on a method of getting sesame seeds to stick to loaves. Let me try my hand at giving you my method for understanding how it is that our deaths actually engage the power of reconciliation—at explaining my theology, if you will, of how the disposal of ourselves is the only way to perfect our disposition.

One preliminary distinction, though. As I have insisted all along, the truth of that is a matter of faith, not proof. It is something you accept because you decide to take someone's word for it, not because you reason your way to it by evidence. And to be frank, the someone whom I have in this case decided to trust is Jesus. About that, you and I may or may not be of one mind. Even if we're not, we can still sit and reason together about how it might work, if, however improbably, it should indeed turn out to be true. For it is such a hilariously good piece of news that, true or not, it's simply a pleasure to talk about it.

Theology is to faith, you see, rather what sesame seeds are to breadmaking. It's not the main thing; but it's such a nice thing to do with the main thing that even people who won't eat bread have been known to lick their fingers and eat up all the toasted seeds that fell from the master loaf. Herewith, therefore, some theological crumbs.

Think, if you will, of your life. And think, please, only of the time between your birth and your death. Theologically, it is just as unnecessary for us to trouble ourselves with your so-called life after death as it is to spend time on your even more problematical life before birth. For whether the times of our pilgrimage here prove to be three score years and ten or three minutes and ten seconds, God holds all those times, long or short, in an eternal hand. As he has their lives, the baby who lives for only a day and the man who dies at a hundred both have eternal lives. As the psalmist says, *their times are in his hands:* whether they flourished for a minute or a century, all that they did, and all that they were, is with him forever.

But on the other hand (quite literally), there is a second grip on your life: your own. That one does have some limitations God's grip does not. For one thing, it is a temporal grasp, not an eternal one. God holds the septuagenarian's days all at once in an everlasting *now*; the old man had to be content to deal with them one at a time. Worse yet, if they were past or future days, they were, on any particular today, impossible for him to grasp at all except in memory or anticipation.

But worst of all, no matter what sort of days they were in terms of time, they were not the best of days in terms of life. If they were days of joy, they were also days of sorrow; if of pleasure, also pain; and if of love, then of anger, jealousy, pride and betrayal as well. And worse than worst, they were days about which his grip was able to do next to nothing. The good of them could not be dependably held, and the evil of them was almost entirely beyond repair. He lived, day to day, in an effort to dispose his times aright; but on any given day they were one vast indisposition in his hands.

Go back now, however, to God's grip upon our days— and to what God's Word says about his holding of them. In the end, when the Scriptures talk about the way he ultimately has the whole world in his hands, it insists that he has it all reconciled—that is, he holds it not as indisposed, but as disposed into the order and beauty it always sought but never found. The Old Testament speaks of the peaceable kingdom where the wolf and the kid lie down together and the sucking child plays upon the hole of the asp. And in the New, the last vision is of the kingdoms of this world transformed into the kingdom of our God and of his Christ—of the heavenly Jerusalem descending, without spot or wrinkle like a bride adorned for her husband. We are promised, in short, a wedding party that goes on forever without a tear.

The question therefore comes: how does he manage that? Where have all the indisposed, unreconciled days of yesteryear gone? What has he done to keep them from giving everybody indigestion at the Supper of the Lamb?

And the answer is: he does it by death. First of all, by the death of Christ. The world God loves—the world that, to its joy and his, he holds in his hands—is the world he sees in his only begotten and beloved Son. That Son, that Word who was the Christ, disposed the world into the Father's hands by creating it; and when it indisposed itself, he redisposed it by taking all its ugliness down into his death, and bringing up only its beauty in his resurrection.

But second, he does it by our death. For, having renewed his grip upon our days by the death and resurrection of Jesus, he now invites us simply to let go of our own grip and enjoy his:

"All that thy child's mistake fancies as lost
Is stored for thee at home
Rise, clasp my hand, and come."

We can safely do that because he has us; and we can do it gladly because he has us reconciled. Our grip is a loser's grip; his is a winner's. On the day that we finally let go altogether, we win, hands down.

There are three corollaries to add to that, all of which bear nicely on remarriage.

The first is that on any day—even before we finally let go of all our days—we are separated from the enjoyment of God's grip upon our days by only one thing: a wall of unbelief. On this side of it, we hold ourselves in our own grip and, to our great and endless discomfort, can do next to nothing with our times. But on the other side of it, he holds us too, and has our times renewed. In other words, all that stands between us and our reconciliation is the life that we, in our incredulity, insist on hanging onto. It is as if a father kept trying to put a delicate gift into a child's hand, and the child insisted on grasping it, instead of receiving it palm open. The minute we stop trying to hold, we have. All because he had us all along. It is quite safe to die, in a remarriage as in anything else. Our life is just on the other side of our unbelieving attempts at living.

Which leads to the second corollary. If this believed truth really is the truth, then the reconciliation on the other side of unbelief is available to anyone who is willing to die, regardless of whether anyone else is willing to or not. The rule, in remarriage as elsewhere, is: the first one to die wins. Is your former husband still lively in his insistence that the two of you are unreconciled? Does your former wife invite you constantly still to live at odds? If they do, that is sad for them. But if you believe that in God's grip all those indispositions are over—and that they are over *now*, because his hands hold all of us now—then you can lay hold of what he holds any time you're willing to die. It's there. And the minute anybody lets go, it's there with power. Therefore, don't wait. Die first and you'll be home sooner.

The last corollary brings us to the last step. If you must not wait to die, you must also not stop being dead. So often we get home by dying, only to forget how we got there. Resurrection occurs not after death, but out of it; just as creation proceeds not after, but out of nothing. All God needs to create a world is zero; and all he needs to reconcile one is the constant offering of the emptiness of our death. He does not make us out of a clutter of pre-existent junk, and he does not redeem us except out of the uncluttered nothing of a life let go.

"Let it go," therefore, is to the new creation the same word of power that "Let there be" was to the old. And as the creative word was spoken not once but always, so must the redeeming one be. Don't wait, therefore, but above all, don't stop. There's a new life coming every time you die.

But as I promised, that will be all of that. If God had meant theologians to talk beyond this point, he would not have brought Madeleine's car into the driveway just now, nor wafted the smell of baking bread out of the kitchen. I shall take my own advice and die, on the spot, to the whole subject.

Now. If you will be so kind as to fetch the wine jug . . .

XXI

AND ON THE THIRD DAY

No, I am not breaking my promise. It's just that now, after all those intervening hours of sipping, cooking and eating, I have an urge to take you for a walk outside the house. We have had, while we talked, nearly the full range of weather here today: an Indian summery morning, a blustery fall afternoon and now, by the looks of it, a clear, almost wintry night. Slip on your coat and come along.

If I made a point this morning of introducing you to the quiet of this place, I should round out the day by showing you something just as remarkable. The silence, of course, is long gone: you will hear the sound of cars in the background for a good couple of hours yet; but out here in the backyard, I invite you to look up at a sky undiminished by any glow of ground light whatsoever. When it gets dark here, it gets dark; the nearest street lamps are on the other side of the island, and what lights are on in the house all face the other way.

I told you at the beginning that I lived by the light and had little use for clocks. But looking up now at the moon and the stars, all of which have moved inexorably from where they were last night, it occurs to me that perhaps one small dent in my promise might be pardoned. For these lights, even more than the sun, make me see time in another way.

Back when it first occurred to me that clock time had gotten a stranglehold on my existence, I assumed that if I could make a break with it, life would become a pattern of high times and timeless moments. Time would not pass or press. Now, though, having lived through three years' worth of changing moons and shifting stars, I find that isn't true at all. If anything, the time-fetteredness of my life is more obvious than ever before. With clock time, you can at least pretend to stop it or ignore it. You can even, by playing games like daylight saving, create and destroy it. But you can't do anything with the night sky.

E pur si muove. Still, it moves. And what it tells me is not that it's going somewhere, but that I am. After I have seen whatever number of moons I shall see, I shall be gone into the nothing out of which I came. Night after night, every time I see one wax or wane, I know that more clearly.

But far from being depressed by it, I find it hopeful in the extreme. If all the things I have said about dying, and letting go and getting myself out of the way should happen to be true, then I am going to make it, no matter what. Whether I wait too long to die, or stop being dead too soon or even if I never start to die at all, I eventually will be dead, and my times finally out of my hands. But because they are already in better hands than mine, I sense a care behind all that inexorability. My life as it is in the resurrection on the third day is also mine now in the inevitable dying of the second day—and the night sky makes me bold to believe it.

I wouldn't, therefore, have missed this second day for the world. Otherwise, I would just have missed the world.